CITIZEN SLAVE

CITIZEN SLAVE

UNDERSTANDING LAW AND LIBERTY

ROBERT HART

Order this book online at www.trafford.com
or email orders@trafford.com

Most Trafford titles are also available at major online book retailers.

Printed in the United States of America.

ISBN: 978-1-4907-4764-4 (sc)
ISBN: 978-1-4907-4765-1 (e)

Trafford rev. 02/09/2015

 www.trafford.com

North America & international
toll-free: 1 888 232 4444 (USA & Canada)
fax: 812 355 4082

Contents

Epigraph

THE FLAMES OF FREEDOM

Smoldering freedom hanging by a thread.
Hidden by delusions of false liberty.
The thin thread unraveling.
Flames struggling to stay alive.
The flicker of freedom's flames dance in the shadows.
Only to be seen by the blind eye.
Most can barely see her faint glow.
Off in the darkness so far away.
There is a sad tear from those who have known her.
Although long forgotten.
Her importance ignored.
Others never caring.
Only the delusions of false liberty are seen now.
Throwing their shadows into darkness.
The light of her great fire once filled my forgotten country.
We were warm with her honor and benevolence.
Integrity filled the air.
If I knew you better, I would know what to do.
I would know where you are.
I would know where to go.
I feel I have lost my way.
If I could just follow your flickering light to guide me?
I will follow it faithfully.
I will not be strayed by deceptive delusions.
I will make a promise I intend to keep.
Guide me into the flames of freedom so I may feel the splendor.
Look! I can see her now.

The flickers growing to flames.
Flames licking off the glowing coals of liberty.
The fresh air of happiness fanning the fire.
Let's grow free of deceptive delusions.
We will cast them off to shine her glorious light.
Let's go into this fire and become one.
Let the flames fill us.
Can you feel the warmth of honor filling the air?
The sense of dignity?
Do you see her now?
I'm here, knocking on the door.
I don't hear a sound!
Is anyone there?

PREFACE

I was compelled to write this book for many different reasons, but there was one reason in particular that was my driving force. Throughout the years I have witnessed the liberties and property of many good, honest, hardworking people being unjustly deprived, extorted and punished by government with no real recourse left to them. I found this to be completely unacceptable in this "so called" free country.

Other compelling inspirations began when I read the books "Common Sense" by Thomas Paine and "Two Treatises of Government" by John Locke. Both books were written centuries ago and inspired great revolutions in history. After I read those books, I realized that there were no modern day books like those of Paine and Locke that address today's current situations and injustices. There are many books that talk about the problems, but there are no books that accurately advocate the solutions to the problems. Just knowing what the problems are is only half the battle. The key is learning and implementing the solutions to the problems.

In my early years of investigating the concepts of personal sovereignty and liberty, I studied with many different private law groups consisting of people from all walks of life. Our focus was understanding law and protecting liberties. We would periodically have meetings to share, discuss and learn different aspects of law and liberty. These studies were very informative, eye opening and patriotic. It gave us great insight into many of today's current problems that we were not able to learn elsewhere.

As a result of understanding what I perceived at that time to be law, I spent many years suing government on different civil rights issues. There were many long nights of preparing pleadings and motions. In my days in the courtroom, I was generally made to feel as if I was in the Hells Angels Club House complaining about one of their favorite biker members. As a pro-se litigator, I was definitely not part of "their Club". I was always quietly amazed at how the attorneys and judges would joke around with each other in the court rooms. It was common for most to hang out together, play golf and attend parties. Most knew each other. Generally speaking, the judge is the attorney's boss in the courtroom.

Patrick Henry was right when he said: *"I predict that we will eventually live under judicial tyranny",* as judicial tyranny is in full force and effect in our courtrooms today. As a result of all that time, money and energy spent, I acquired real life experiences and understandings of our judicial system.

There came a time in my life when the study of law became so in depth and complicated that one night I sat back and said: *"No one should have to study this much and know all these things merely to protect their God given rights and liberties in a free country! Something is wrong here!"* Shortly after that rousing moment, all of the years of study and lawsuits gelled in my mind and the principles of real law rooted into my understanding. That understanding instilled in me a sovereign mentality and I became a "free man".

The acquisition of my new understanding of "real law" was like any activity that you practice frequently and it becomes second nature and commonplace. I realized that real law was simple and meant to be easily understood by anyone of common understanding and intelligence. Law was created by the people, for the people. The law was never meant to be complicated. Otherwise it would obviously be unjust as it has evolved today.

It has been very disheartening as well as personally motivating to witness how the judicial system tricks and intimidates litigants into not understanding or using real law. The legal tactics in today's court rooms are mostly procedural maneuverings. Lawful principles have very little to do with anything in our judicial system today. The procedural law that is practiced by attorneys is a mere perversion of real law. As you will learn herein, Law trumps Procedure.

I find it almost comical that the entire concept of law has been subsequently manipulated to "appear" so complicated that only skilled attorneys and judges are capable of understanding law. My many conversations with judges and attorneys has led me to believe that they arrogantly believe this to be true. They appear to actually believe the ridiculous concept that a person must have a license to understand law, justice and moral social interaction. To this day I have failed to have even one comprehensive intelligent conversation about law with a judge or attorney. For some reason they avoid it like the plague. I think they believe it would be legal blasphemy to have such a conversation or they just don't want to make a fool out of themselves. One attorney actually admitted to me: *"You probably know more about law than I do as we were only taught two weeks of law in law school. The rest of our training was all about learning procedure."*

These legal tricks, illusions and special favors have brought our once great "free country" to its knees by forced unjust obligations and punishments upon the people. It is actually a hidden despotism hiding under the red, white and blue. These stealthy legal illusions have stolen the rights, liberties and property from countless millions of good people under the guise of what is good for their country, misguided patriotic duty and what only appears to be law. This trickery has always been the ways of the tyrants and those that wish to control others. The only reason this trickery works is because of the ignorance of most people and legal professionals to understand real law.

I subsequently tempered my studies with common sense and started looking at the subject of law in a totally new way. The way law was understood and practiced in earlier times. The simplicity of law is right in front of us all the time. We just find it illusive to break through our different forms of modern day mind control (preconceived ideas) to see the truth. Once you strip away the mind control, it becomes almost funny how you couldn't see the truth before. It becomes hilariously obvious like: "Why did it take so long to put wheels on suitcases?"

I have been blessed with the knowledge and understanding to present the subject of real law to people in a way that was meant to be easily understood. The way the law was originally intended. It is not rocket science. It is simple, commonplace and ordinary. It is "the law of the people, for the people."

I'm sure you will find it exciting to learn and apply these common sense methods of understanding "the law of the people". There is a quote from Confucius: *"Real knowledge is to know the extent of one's ignorance".* When the people finally realize what law really is, the change will come. Step by step, inch by inch, person by person, case by case. Like water running down a hill, it will be unstoppable because knowledge is true power. We built all of our great civilizations on a framework of knowledge.

I am quite confident that someday all people will understand real law from childhood to grave. The only question is when? Our society will eventually understand law with the same ease and importance as we read, write and perform math. It is the missing link in our current society. It is the keystone to a successful civilization. When that time comes, our society will finally evolve with benevolent and moral intelligence. Then we will eliminate wars and injustice once and for all. Only those who create injustice will be prosecuted for their willful acts of violating the rights of others.

We are now on the precipice. We are on the edge looking down into that confusing dark crevasse of accepted injustice. We will either educate ourselves and take control of our personal liberties and governments, or we will fall head first into the depths of accepted, unjust, concealed despotism. If we do fall down that crevasse, it will be a long, steep, slippery climb back up. It may be the fall of no return. With the destructive technological power and military might of government, it may be impossible to ever come back to true freedom.

The following facts are very motivational for me: Most citizens, subjects, serfs and slaves throughout history accepted whatever their masters, kings and rulers inflicted upon them. Most all of those who resisted were crushed and their knowledge buried or hidden. Most all believed there was nothing they could do to stop the forced obligations imposed on them. That's the routine. That's the historical pattern. Are we ready to break these patterns?

America is the last vestige of freedom in the world. If America goes down, the whole world goes down with her. America is being dismantled so slowly and incrementally that nobody notices. The spirits of our forefathers are beseeching us to "wake up"!

The first step is to understand real law and then we will as a civilization, instinctively demand that our rights are respected by proclaiming: "Prove you have the right to infringe upon my liberties."

True Freedom and Liberty must prevail if the people are to evolve to the next level of humanity.

INTRODUCTION

This book is a step-by-step instruction manual for understanding and repairing America's government and re-instituting the sovereign rights of the people. Just as the time, place, and conditions were right to plant the seeds of liberty in the formation of America, so now are the conditions ripe to save that endangered tree of liberty which has grown from those sacred seeds.

Now is the time to nurture this sacred tree of liberty back to vibrant health and to plant anew, worldwide forests of the trees of liberty, which will never again become forgotten or endangered.

Just as the art of reading and writing have impacted humanity, so will the workings and understanding of freedom, liberty and common law become ingrained in the minds and lives of the people so they will never again fall into peril as long as man can reason and has the righteousness to see justice prevail.

> *"Enlighten the people generally, and tyranny and oppressions of the body and mind will vanish like evil spirits at the dawn of day."*
>
> **Thomas Jefferson**

The subject matter of this book will enlighten the reader to a full understanding and realization of the free and sovereign mentality on which America was founded. To acquire a free sovereign mentality, one must have a full understanding of personal sovereignty, natural law, freedom, liberty, and the failure of the free people of America and the world to rebut the presumptions of positive law and legal trickery that have enslaved them without their knowledge. This book will guide the reader step by step into this free sovereign mentality, for the betterment of America and all mankind.

Although this book is written with Americans in mind, its subject matter is applicable to all people in all countries. The principles propounded in this book are maxims of logical thought, truth, and law that have been put together in a simple-to-understand and enlightening format for the benefit of the common man and society as a whole.

> *"It is a piece of idle sentimentality that truth, merely as truth, has any inherent power denied to error, of prevailing. . . . The real advantage which truth has consists in this, that when an opinion is true, it may be extinguished once, twice, or many times, but in the course of ages there will generally be found persons to rediscover it, until some one of its reappearances falls on a time when from favorable circumstances it escapes persecution until it has made such head as to withstand all subsequent attempts to suppress it."*
>
> **John Stuart**

Most readers will recognize each concept of this book as truth and common sense, though they have never been able to put all the truths together to form the big picture. It is as though the majority of people have been looking at many pieces of a jigsaw puzzle for many years. The puzzle pieces have been scattered haphazardly over the table all of their lives. They know each piece with intimacy and can recognize each at a glance. Yet, as familiar as they are with each piece, they have never put all the pieces together to see the entire assembled picture of the puzzle.

The following pages will allow readers of all ages and walks of life to put these important pieces together in order to see one of the most important pictures of all time. This is a true picture of the salvation and protection of the most precious yet overlooked gift that your creator can give you: our God-given inherent rights and liberties according to natural law, and the ability to protect these precious gifts.

As you read this book, you may notice the puzzle pieces moving closer and closer into position to reveal the final picture. As you notice the picture emerging before you, layers of past-instilled mind control will begin to lift from your consciousness like skins of an onion. When the picture is complete, you will be honored with knowledge that will cause true freedom, liberty, and sovereignty to flourish in your mentality and life. You will then forever recognize where each piece of the puzzle fits in the big picture. This knowledge will cause the spirits of our forefathers and all past heroes of freedom and liberty to cheer from their sacred graves.

Remember: The truth shall set you free.

Should it finally come to pass that the people of America learn to understand the principles that are communicated in these pages, America will once again become a benevolent and just nation respected by the civilized world.

As you read this text you will receive insights from famous men of the past, as if they were speaking directly to you from the heavens. These famous quotes should be a reminder that the long-forgotten principles rekindled in these pages were once common place among all people. It is truly an honor to learn from these famous men.

Hopefully your re-enlightenment will cause you to understand that the problems America and the world are experiencing now are due to the complacency of the people toward understanding and protecting the precious gifts of freedom and liberty. Believe it or not, it is up to you. It is up to all individuals to protect their own rights and liberties. So read the words of our forefathers and understand that each of us can and will make a difference. We will then change the entire world for the better and move humanity to the next step in human and social evolution.

May the spirit of all lovers of mankind, freedom, and liberty, ride beside you on this journey into sovereign enlightenment.

> *"The object of the superior man is truth."*
> **Confucius**

The Broken Machine

W hen you think of America, you think of freedom, liberty, and justice for all. We all love our country. Many Americans feel that they would fight and die for our country and our American way of life. People in other countries desire to come to America because of the principles of freedom and liberty with which America was founded and supposedly stands for today.

America is the only country that was founded on the principle that all people are free sovereign individuals with no master, king, or dictator. The American people are supposed to be their own kings and masters of their own lives, with no one to rule their lives but themselves. Even the poor should hold full title to their lands, homes, and possessions without being forced into involuntary servitude or having rights taken away by force.

During the eighteenth century when America was forming, the concepts of true freedom and liberty were well ingrained in the mentality of the population. That is why the people of America desired to sever ties with the King of England. They needed no man to rule their lives. They needed to work for no one but for whom they freely chose to work, whether it was themselves or someone else. They fully understood the maxim of law that no one could force an obligation upon another with impunity. It was this free-thinking spirit that sparked the formation of the greatest and most powerful country in the world.

But something has gone drastically wrong, and it has slowly changed America, like a glacier slowly moving down the mountain side without notice. Americans now have only the illusion of the principles of freedom and liberty upon which their country was founded. People are being forced to supply their hard-earned money and labor for taxes, licenses, permits, fees, and a host of other presumed obligations. People are losing their homes, farms, businesses, possessions, families, and freedoms because of obligations that are being forced upon them in the name of what is good for the country. The people do not refuse these forced obligations under threat of punishment, loss of possessions, or out of ignorance or misguided patriotism for America. It is as though the people of America are living under the control of a hidden king or dictator rather than under the original intent of our free American society and government.

> *"Because of what only appears to be a lawful command on the surface, many citizens, because of their respect for what only appears to be law, are cunningly coerced into waiving their rights, due to ignorance."*
> **U.S. Supreme Court in U.S. vs Minker, 350 U.S. 179 at 187**

Although the end result of these forced obligations is exactly the same as in any feudal kingdom or dictatorship, most people are in denial and still believe the propaganda that America is a free country. In one breath they claim they are free and in the next breath they pay their hard-earned labor to the tax man. The only difference is that the controlling authorities in America are not called kings or dictators. America's dictator/king is hidden from view of the people.

Although the everyday lives of the people are controlled exactly the same as if they were under the control of a king or dictator, the people are fed the same mantra over and over: "You are free and you live in the freest country in the world." The rules and regulations that are forcing the private people to work overtime for their hidden master have encroached so slowly over the years that no one even noticed as it happened. The tentacles of the great invisible octopus of oppression and tyranny have finally secured its grip upon the good people of America. All those who attempt to break this all-powerful grip will be surely punished and silenced for questioning the great authority of our hidden American King.

And there are those who will say, "We live in the freest and best country in the world!" Such people do not fully understand freedom. And if this is true, it only means that the rest of the world must be in really bad shape. Sure, you can always live in the best cell in the prison, or the best house in the ghetto, but that does not mean that you cannot improve what you have left.

> *"Good intentions will always be pleaded for any assumption of power. The Constitution was made to guard the people against the dangers of good intentions. There are men in all ages who mean to govern well, but they mean to govern. They promise to be good masters, but they mean to be masters."*
>
> **Daniel Webster**

People all over America are asking the same questions more and more each year:

Why do I have to work a certain amount of time just to pay the government?

When will they ever stop increasing all these fees and taxes?

Why do I feel like I have no say in the demands my government is putting on me?

If America is a free country, why does so much of my hard-earned labor go to the government?

Why am I required to pay these ever-increasing taxes?

Why am I required to pay all these licenses, permits, and insurance fees?

If I own my home, how can they seize my property if I fail to pay property tax or abide by building codes?

How can they fine me and throw me in jail for things I do that have damaged no one?

How can they force my child to take drugs like Ritalin, Dexedrine, and other harmful drugs and punish me if I refuse?

How can they take my children from me and break up my family?

Why is my voice not heard in court unless I hire an attorney?

How can they confiscate my car if I have created no injury and not infringed upon the rights of anyone?

Why do I feel like I'm always violating some obscure written law?
Isn't involuntary servitude and debtors' prison unlawful in America?
Why does it seem that if I have no money, I have very few or no rights?
Why can police kill innocent people and get away with it?
Why do I need money to protect myself in a court of law?
What's going on in America?
Where is the justice in America?
Why can I not receive fair due process of law in our court systems?

> *"If we do not maintain Justice, Justice will not maintain us."*
> **Francis Bacon**

Americans are starting to realize that something is very wrong in our so-called free country. There are situations occurring at an alarming rate in which the following question has emerged: "How could something like this happen in this free country?" People are being imprisoned when they have caused no damage. Properties are being seized under the pretense of forced presumed agreements. People are being forced to pay debts that have been forced upon them without just cause, without agreement, and without their consent. In most cases, the victims are without the sufficient resources to effectively fight back, wanting only for the situation to go away and not come back. In almost all cases the people are simply left without a realistic and fair remedy, as the courts have turned a deaf ear and a blind eye to the common people unless they hire an attorney. Even with legal representation people are forced to capitulate to the forced obligations.

The sad part about these situations is that the people that can afford to pay the forced obligations subliminally consider them as some kind of business expense and do not really consider them a usurpation of their freedoms or liberties. Only when punishment and court action ensues do they begin to feel the grip of this hidden tyranny. But by this time it is usually too late to learn what their rights really are and they are merely forced to comply and/or hire an attorney.

The poor people and people who live on a shoe-string (that is most Americans) feel the usurpation of their rights immediately because the forced obligations steal their labor, time, and money, which they need for their families and survival. These people usually have no money to hire attorneys and feel the full wrath of America's hidden king/dictator. And just like the rich folks, the poor are ignorant of how and why it can even happen in America: they only know that it does. So they figure out ways to hide from the tyranny and pay only that from which they cannot escape.

Ask most people why they pay their taxes and the majority will respond, "Well, we just have to." "If we don't they will punish us by stealing our property, possessions, and pay checks, or throw us in jail." Does this sound like people living in a free country?

The natural rights of the good people of America have been stealthily encroached upon by a government that continuously convinces the people that "their freedoms and liberties are protected and that they live in the freest country in the world. "Love it or leave it" it seems to say.

As a cunning thief would steal merchandise from a blind and trusting store clerk, our government has tricked the good patriotic people of America into involuntary servitude without their ever knowing of the theft. Loyal Americans have been tricked into believing that whatever rights or property they may give up is "for the good of the country," or they believe that "if we don't capitulate we won't have roads or schools." Every oppressive ruler in history has had good-sounding excuses for the forced obligations it has imposed on its subjects.

> *"The genius of our ruling class is that it has kept a majority of the people from ever questioning the inequity of a system where most people drudge along, paying heavy taxes for which they get nothing in return."*
> **Gore Vidal**

The majority of Americans have forgotten that the principles of true freedom, liberty, and personal sovereignty are the founding principles of our American way of life. Freedom, liberty, and sovereignty is what made America different from all other countries in the history of the world. It is what made America the most prosperous and greatest country in the world. Our freedoms have been plucked from us one feather at a time until finally we are standing in the cold wondering how it came to be.

But we must all be aware of one all-important fact. If we as a people continue to allow the erosion of our personal freedoms, our country will become no better than all the feudal governments from which our founding fathers risk all to free our country from. The seizing and controlling of our natural rights are destructive to the founding principles and moral bedrock of this great nation. Any time you undermine the foundation of anything, the structure will eventually crumble.

America is the example to the whole world. If we do not save our country now from falling into complete blatant feudalism, it will not only affect the American people and our posterity forever, but negatively affect the freedom of the entire world. It is up to all of us to cause the tides of change to save our country.

So what can we do? The natural order of life tells us continuously that all of the great answers to all of the great questions will be revealed in the simplest possible form. This pattern of life proves itself over and over. The following pages of this book will describe what the real hidden problems are and the simple solutions to the problems. Yes, it is a simple solution. Knowledge and the ability to reason is what have caused humans to be the possessors of the world. This same knowledge and logic will cause true freedom and liberty to ring again.

> *"It is not the function of our government to keep the citizen from falling into error; it is the function of the citizen to keep the government from falling into error."*
> **U.S. Supreme Court, in American Communications Association *vs* Douds.**

Just as a magician will have you looking at one thing when you should actually be looking at something else, our legal system has tricked society in the same manner. By reading this book, you will learn what you should be looking at, instead of what you believe you should be looking at. People tend to do things the way they have always done out of habit and without thinking. This is just human nature. Even the simplest task seems difficult to those who are new to the task. For example, reading would be impossible without learning the alphabet. But once the simple task is learned, it becomes easy and commonplace and can be used effectively without thinking. This book will reveal to all people who are interested in becoming a free sovereign people again, the simple principles that will allow people to easily and simply conduct their lives in a manner that protects their freedoms and liberties.

Remember, if you fail to protect your liberties, then you do not deserve them, as you yourself have contributed to the undermining of the founding principles of America. Yes it is true, you actually have to get up off your butt and protect what you value as sacred. No one is going to do it for you. Yes, you have to be responsible for your own actions, or inactions.

> *"A man cannot part with his liberty and have it too, convey it by compact to the magistrate, and retain it himself."*
> **John Locke**

The problems we are talking about are caused by a long evolution of deception that has crept into the private lives of the people over many years. This deception was able to take place due to a few simple factors:

1. The ignorance of the people concerning what is actually happening to them
2. The complacency, fear, or financial insufficiency which prevents the people from fighting against the all-powerful intimidation of ever-aggressing government agencies
3. The propaganda that if we do not give up our rights we are unpatriotic and the country will go broke
4. The belief of the general public that an individual's rights are subject to the will of the legislature

But just like the all-powerful Oz in the movie The Wizard of Oz, the all powerful intimidating force becomes inept once you pull back the curtain to expose the fraud and deception. When the people educate themselves about what is actually happening to them, then the deception can deceive no more. And you can be assured that the knowledge to free the people is so simple and so obvious that it will be easily learned and understood by all of society. The answer is as easy as learning to read. Just as we learned the alphabet in order to read and write, we learn to understand the basics of law in order to understand law, justice, and personal sovereignty. Knowledge is truly power.

> **"Real knowledge is to know the extent of one's ignorance."**
> **Confucius**

The subject matter in this book is as important to the average American as knowing how to swim is to a surfer, or knowing how to read a map is to a traveler. Imagine a foolish surfer who feels that he does not need to know how to swim because he is leashed to his floating surfboard. It is just a matter of time before he falls off his surfboard, his leash breaks, and he is left to the mercy of the uncaring ocean.

Many people as well are left to the mercy of the uncaring "system" because of their ignorance of what is actually taking place. When they are at the mercy of the system, they feel helpless about what to do. Usually their only hope is to have the financial capability to hire an attorney, if indeed an attorney can or will help in the particular circumstance. Many times hiring an attorney just makes things worse by causing more financial debt, hardship, and vulnerability. There are many times when people are simply left without a realistic and fair means to procure justice. Which means that due process of law has been denied to the people.

It is the object of this book to bring into the consciousness of the reader a true understanding of freedom, liberty, the basic rights of man, and the protection of the natural rights and liberties of all free people.

The cause of freedom and liberty for the people of America is the same cause of all mankind in all countries and governments. Even animals strive to be free. It is a universal truth and desire that stretches across all boundaries, to all people, of all times. Freedom and liberty is supposed to be the end result of law and justice.

The organized truths asserted in these pages are maxims of logical thought that are self-evident to all people of logical and rational reasoning. These maxims cannot be questioned by anyone of honest and sane reflection.

> *"We hold these truths to be self-evident, that all men are created equal, that they are endowed by their Creator with certain unalienable Rights that among these are Life, Liberty, and the pursuit of Happiness."*
> **Thomas Jefferson**

How We Learn to Obey Our Masters

We must exam why some people feel they must be subservient to their government or that somehow their government has power over their lives.

It is a psychological condition or form of mind control that has been instilled since birth and through many generations. Many people believe that their government will cause good things to happen in their lives and keep them safe. People want to be loyal to their government without really realizing what their government actually is. They tend to confuse government with their country and countrymen. It is a kind of illusion where people generally do not investigate the actual truth of what their government is really up to.

Up until the age of the internet the only thing you knew about your government was what you saw on the nightly news broadcast or in the newspaper. We now know that the mainstream news is basically a government propaganda network specifically designed to instill whatever form of mind control the government wants the populace to believe.

But the big question is why the people tend to blindly believe what their government tells them even in the face of outright facts that would contradict the government's propaganda.

> *"One of the greatest delusions in the world is the hope that the evils in this world are to be cured by legislation."*
> **Thomas B. Reed**

It is very common to find people that get angry if someone shows them facts that might contradict their erroneous beliefs in their government. It is commonly called blind loyalty where you are for your government whether they are right or wrong. It is common to see whole populations swayed into hating or persecuting a certain group of people because of what they heard on the news or from the government propaganda network. This can be very serious and dangerous and has caused untold strife and wars in the past.

> **"Facts do not cease to exist because they are ignored."**
> **Aldous Huxley**

How could whole populations be so easily swayed into propaganda and untruths? Let's take a look at a real life situation which will shed some light on how people have become conditioned to accept involuntary servitude.

The following true story reflects real life situations that happen to thousands of people in America every day. The names have been changed at the request of the people this story is about. This true story starts out about a guy named Jack and how he came to understand the most important aspects of his freedoms and liberties.

When Jack was born he was completely dependant on his parents for survival. By natural law it was the responsibility of Jack's parents to ensure his survival until he reached the age in which he could reason for himself and survive on his own.

As Jack was growing up, he was bound by natural law to obey his parents. There was certain family rules that Jack was required to obey. For all practical purposes, Jack's parents were his masters, and rightly so when speaking of children. If Jack disobeyed his parents, they could punish him. Jack learned quickly in life that if he obeyed the rules of the family, good things would happen. When he disobeyed or questioned his parent's authority, bad things happened.

Jack's very first perception of life started in a feudal society in which he was subservient to his masters (his parents). This was of course, for his own good, as he was a child and could not survive on his own in the world.

Before Jack entered school, he was subservient to most adults in his life. When he started school, he became subservient to his teachers and the written rules and regulations of the school. Jack essentially had a new set of masters to obey. If he disobeyed his teachers or these written rules and regulations, he was punished for doing so. Just as in his family structure, Jack learned that when he obeyed the rules of school, he would not be punished and good things would happen to him.

> *"A journey of a thousand miles begins with a single step."*
> **Confucius**

As the years past, Jack started playing sports after school. He learned quickly that it was to his best advantage to obey the commands of his coach and the rules of the game. Jack added a new master to his list of current masters. If he disobeyed his coach or the rules of the game, he would sit on the bench or be punished. Jack reinforced the concepts of abiding by the written rules for the activity in which he was involved. He learned quickly that when he obeyed the rules, good things happened to him.

When Jack became sixteen he wanted to own and drive a car. There were certain rules which Jack's parents had lain down that he was required to obey in order to get permission from his parents to have a car. Jack had to get a part time job to pay for his car.

Jack found a job. Now Jack had another new master: his boss. Jack knew that he must obey the rules of his job and his boss or he would not be able to make the money to buy the car he wanted. Jack learned quickly that if he obeyed all the rules of his job and his boss, good things would happen to him.

When Jack received his first pay check he learned that he had acquired another new master which had control over the money he got paid. This new master was called the IRS. Jack was told that he must pay some of the money he earned to the IRS in the form of income taxes. Jack learned through word of mouth that he must always pay part of his earnings to the IRS throughout his entire life or the IRS would punish him. Jack accepted the IRS as one of his masters because by this time he was used to having many masters in his life and he did not know anything about legislative laws. Jack was told that the IRS would punish him if he did not obey their rules. By this time, Jack was so used to taking on masters without question that he accepted his latest new master. He learned quickly that if he obeyed the IRS and did not question its authority, he would not be punished.

> *"When the government violates the people's rights, insurrection is for the people and for each portion of the people, the most sacred of rights and the most indispensable of duties."*
> **Lafayette**

Jack was able to buy his car, and went to the Department of Motor Vehicles (DMV) to get his driver's license and registration. He learned that he had to accept yet another master and a whole new set of written rules to abide by. Jack was required to pass written and driving tests to get his license. Once he received his license, he was instructed that he must register his car and obey all the rules of the road or his driver's license would be taken away and he would not be permitted to drive his own vehicle. This new master was one of the most powerful masters because this one had authority over Jack's ability to get from one place to another conveniently.

Jack was told that he must comply with orders from any police officer that might pull him over, or he would be taken to jail. Jack did not understand the written laws pertaining to traffic, but he did understand the concept of punishment and jail. Jack took for granted that the police knew what they were doing and that his compliance with any order from a police officer must be the right thing to do, especially since police officers carried guns and could throw Jack in jail. Remember that he had been trained from earliest childhood to obey "the rules" and whoever was his master at the time. Jack had been conditioned since birth that if he obeyed the rules he would not be punished.

Up to this point, Jack had many masters in his pre-adult lifetime. He had his parents, grandparents, big brother and sister, teachers, principals, coaches, bosses, IRS, DMV, and police officers. His childhood had been nothing but complying with the wishes and demands of his many masters. But Jack knew one thing for sure: he lived in America and America stood for freedom and liberty. Jack knew that he was totally free as long as he obeyed all of his masters.

Now Jack was nearing young adulthood. He had graduated high school and was ready to start learning how to become successful in life. Jack decided that he wanted to join the military so he could have money for college and loans to buy a house. He joined the military, and for the next four years he had a new master: the military. Jack was now a young adult and was fully subject to the written military rule. He was for the most part, controlled by written rules in every aspect of his life. Along with his military masters, Jack was told that his private life was subject to laws called statutes that were enacted by the legislature. Jack had never been trained to understanding legislative law, but he took for granted that if it was a law, then he must obey it. Jack had learned throughout his life that when he obeyed the law he would not be punished.

> *"Always do right. This will gratify some people, and astonish the rest."*
>
> **Mark Twain**

Jack got out of the military and wanted to go to college. First, though, he was required to comply with the rules and regulations that governed the payment of Jack's school tuition money that he earned in the military. He complied with these written rules and regulations and started college. Jack was now subject to all of the written rules and regulations of the college. If he wanted to graduate he had to study hard and abide by all the written rules of his college. Jack knew from experience that if he abided by all the rules and studied hard, good things would happen to him.

While Jack was attending college, he got a job driving a gravel truck for a local paving company. He was required to pass certain tests and abide by another set of regulations to get his CDL license to drive big trucks.

The pay was good enough for Jack to purchase a small starter home in a residential neighborhood. Jack learned that he had a new master. He would have to pay property tax to the county treasurer. Jack was informed that if he failed to pay the property tax, the local government would take his house away from him and sell it to someone else. Jack had learned from experience that he shouldn't question authority and that if he obeyed all the rules he would not be punished.

Jack sat down one night and figured out that between payroll taxes, property taxes, license fees, registration fees, and mandatory vehicle insurance, he was forced to work a certain number of months per year strictly for the government or be punished for refusing to do so. But Jack still believed that he was a free man in a free country because that was what he had been taught all of his life. America was the land of the free. Jack always loved to say the pledge of allegiance. Jack still believed that he lived in the freest country in the world.

It is safe to say that by this time in Jack's life he was totally conditioned to abide by the written rule. His whole life had been conditioned to abide by masters, rules, laws and regulations. He now believed that the written rule was all there was. Jack had always been told that without written laws, there would be anarchy. Up to this point, Jack had never learned about the common law, natural law, or what maxims of law are. Jack knew the difference between right and wrong, but he believed that right, wrong, and justice was regulated by written enacted laws. He was now firmly convinced that if he obeyed all written laws, freedom, liberty, and justice would prevail. He still believed that he was free even though he was forced to work a good percentage of his life for the government. Jack also believed that others should have to do the same as well. Jack really didn't have time to analysis this subject in depth because his life was busy and he didn't need any trouble in his life.

> *"It is one thing to show a man that he is in an error, and another to put him in possession of truth."*
> **John Lock**

Because Jack had never studied the law or how laws are enacted, he failed to understand that all legislative laws are enacted by Congress, the legislature, or some other lawmaking body. Because Jack had been so conditioned in his life to abide by some presumed higher authority, he never questioned or even wondered whether or not he was even obligated to abide by written laws. Jack never considered the aspect of consent to all these rules and laws. All Jack knew was that if it was a law, he had to abide by it or he would be a law-breaker and a criminal. Jack paid all of his taxes because he had been told that it was the law and that if you broke the law you would go to jail.

Jack had never been taught that all lawmaking bodies have only the limited authority to make rules, regulations, laws, and statutes, which pertain only to the regulation of government and related consenting commercial activities. Because Jack had always had many masters in one form or another, he was conditioned to accept whatever authority appeared to be legitimate.

Throughout Jack's entire life, he had never been taught the basic concepts of true freedom and liberty. The concept of true freedom and liberty had never been taught in school or discussed among friends or family. Jack had never experienced true freedom and liberty in his life because he had always been subject to some form of man-made higher authority. There had always been someone to dictate his conduct. Jack believed he had true freedom and liberty because he could come and go as he pleased as long as he abided by the rules of man-made authority and "paid his fair share."

Something Happened to Jack

One day something happened to Jack that rocked his world. Something happened that popped the bubble in which Jack lived.

A young lady named Lisa, about Jack's age, worked at the local convenience store where he normally got gas and coffee. Jack would usually strike up a friendly conversation with Lisa when he was in the store. She was married to a nice guy named Dave who was a framing carpenter. Lisa and Dave had three wonderful young children and had just moved to town from Alabama, which was very far away. They both had jobs and they scraped by living in a rented three-bedroom house in a poor part of town.

> *"The only fence against the world is a thorough knowledge of it."*
>
> **John Locke**

One day when Jack was in the store he noticed that Lisa was very upset and he asked if anything was wrong. Lisa told Jack that Dave had been pulled over for a routine traffic stop. The cop had searched Dave's truck and had found a baggy of pot and Dave's unregistered pistol under the seat. Dave was arrested on the charges of concealed weapon, unregistered firearm, and possession of pot. Dave was in jail with a large bail. Dave and Lisa barely had enough money on which to survive, let alone money for bail. Lisa exclaimed almost in tears, "Dave hasn't hurt anyone and he is the nicest guy in the world. Why is he in jail? What am I going to do?"

Dave was just a framing carpenter and did not understand the law. All Dave knew was that he was in violation of some kind of laws. He did not understand that those laws he was accused of being in violation of had no authority over him. Dave only knew that he had created no damage or danger to anyone, but he was being unjustly imprisoned.

Dave was the kind of guy that did not drink alcohol, coffee, smoke cigarettes, or do any kind of hard drugs. Dave would only occasionally smoke a little pot at night when he wanted to relax. He enjoyed smoking pot and had smoked it in moderation all of his adult life. Smoking pot was normal for Dave. Pot was Dave's only vice. He believed he had a perfect right to smoke it if he so desired.

Dave also came from the country and believed that he had the right to carry his gun in his car and that it was an invasion of his rights to register his gun with the government. After rumors that the government was attempting to take guns away from the people, the last thing he was going to do was tell the government that he owned a gun and where he kept it. This was his right as an American. Dave believed in the Second Amendment which says, "The right of the people to keep and bear arms shall not be infringed." Besides, he harmed no one by keeping his gun in his truck for protection. Dave and Lisa lived in a bad part of town because they were relatively poor and could not afford high rent. Staying armed was a smart thing to do in their high-crime neighborhood.

> *"Are we at last brought to such humiliating and debasing degradation, that we cannot be trusted with arms for our defense?"*
> **Patrick Henry**

On the day Dave was pulled over he had just acquired some pot from a friend and was taking it home. When the rookie cop pulled Dave over, the computer showed that Dave had been busted for possession of pot two years earlier in Alabama. This cop was in a bad mood and started to hassle Dave and search the truck. Dave had no criminal record except for the pot bust.

Because it was Dave's second offense on the pot charge and the prosecutor was out for blood, Dave was sentenced to a minimum of one year in the county jail on the three charges. This was extremely hard on the young family of five because Lisa could not possibly make it on the salary she made at the convenience store. The young couple had no relatives to fall back on. They were new to town and had no close friends. They were on their own.

> *"Wherever Law ends, Tyranny begins."*
> **John Locke**

A few months later Jack noticed that Lisa was not working in the store anymore. Jack asked the new store clerk what happened to her. He replied that he was new and did not know Lisa or what happened to her, but that he had heard a rumor about someone getting thrown in jail.

Two weeks later Jack saw Lisa sitting on a bus bench. She looked like something was terribly wrong and she appeared in disarray. She was not her usual cheery self and did not have her usual well-kept appearance. He pulled over to say hello and asked her if he could give her a lift somewhere. She looked terribly upset and hopped in Jack's truck. As she held back her tears she began to tell Jack what had happened since they had last talked at the store.

It turned out that Lisa and Dave's truck registration and insurance had come due shortly after Dave was thrown in jail. Lisa, of course, had no money for the registration, let alone the state-required insurance. They had already spent all their savings on issues related to Dave's arrest and conviction. She had already borrowed money for part of the rent, food and clothes for the kids, plus getting the truck out of impound. She had no one left to turn to for financial help. All she could do was work and hope something good would come along. Luckily Lisa got some extra overtime and a neighbor watched the kids for free.

By a stroke of bad luck, Lisa was pulled over and received two citations for expired registration and no insurance. Lisa, raising three children by herself, had no money for registration, insurance, or the fines that would be imposed on her by traffic court. To Lisa, it was a choice between food, rent, and clothes for her kids, or extortion money for the state. She was so busy working and raising the three kids that she had no time to appear in court for the citations. She was never involved in an accident and had a perfect driving record.

Consequently the traffic court put out a bench warrant for her arrest. Lisa was pulled over about a week later while driving to work. The cops arrested Lisa, took her to jail, and impounded her truck. She had no money for bail or impound fees and her three kids were home from school waiting for her. Lisa explained that she became very upset while being booked and explained that she had done nothing to deserve jail time and that she had three young children at home. She desperately explained that she had to get home to take care of her children. "No problem" said someone in booking, "we will send Child Protective Services to the house to take care of the children."

As fate would have it, Lisa had no financial resources for bail or to pay impound fees. The judge gave Lisa twenty days for failing to appear. Consequently she lost her job and her house (she was already late on rent), her truck was impounded, her possessions were put in storage by the landlord, and her kids were hauled off to child haven and put into foster homes. When she finally got out of jail she could not get her kids out of state custody because she had lost her home and had nowhere to live and no way to get the kids to school. Lisa's only recourse was to stay at a women's shelter temporarily. She was emotionally destroyed, not knowing what to do, fighting the government bureaucracy to get her kids back with nowhere to live, all while her husband was in jail. This all happened because their paperwork was not in order and they did not comply with some rule that someone wrote down on a piece of paper which someone called a "law." Dave and Lisa were no threat to society and had damaged no one. They were good, honest people who had fallen prey to the statutory oppression of the state.

> *"The truth is great, and shall prevail when none cares whether it prevail or not."*
> **Coventry Patmore**

Jack was in shock after hearing that such an outrageous chain of events had happened to such good people like Dave and Lisa.

Jack thought that if there were more people in the world like Dave and Lisa, it would be a better place to live. They were some of the nicest law-abiding people he had known. Dave and Lisa were anything but criminals. They were great working-class parents with great kids and a happy life before this all happened. They did not damage or infringe upon anyone, yet their whole life and family was turned upside down by our American government simply because a lawmaker wrote a law on a piece of paper and was presumed that they were subject to obey it. In common law jurisdiction the misery that was inflicted upon this decent young family would have never happened. By the rule of common law, the government is the law breaker. But there is nobody to take the government to jail.

To add irony and hypocrisy to the situation, Jack read in the newspaper that the assistant DA that prosecuted Dave was busted for possession of cocaine while attempting to pick up a hooker downtown. No charges were brought against him apparently because of his political connections at city hall. (He was fired but eventually got his job back a year later.)

> *"The Second Amendment was never intended to allow private citizens to 'keep and bear arms.' If it was, there would have been wording such as 'the right of the People to keep and bear arms shall not be infringed.'"*
> **Ken Konechi**

Jack realized there was no justice done in Dave and Lisa's situation. Jack wondered how something like this could happen in America. Jack always believed that America stood for freedom, liberty, and justice for all. In this situation there was only injustice served from the hands of legislative jurisdiction and a cold, uncaring, destructive government.

For the first time in Jack's life he questioned the authority and validity of the government, which had destroyed Dave and Lisa's life over nothing. Jack dropped Lisa off at the women's homeless shelter, gave her fifty dollars and told her to call him if she needed anything. He would do all he could to help.

Jack was so angry after hearing Lisa's story that he stopped at his local watering hole. He began telling the unbelievable story to a few of his buddies over a game of pool. It became the topic of conversation in the bar that night. To Jack's surprise, other people told Jack similar horror stories that had happened to them. All of the stories involved people who had injured no one, but who were persecuted by the presumed authority of legislative jurisdiction. An old German man in the bar told Jack, "I was only a kid in Nazi Germany, but I never remember it being as bad as this country has become. I remember that Hitler had all the people saying and believing, 'We are the master race'. I notice now that the people are mind controlled in the same way except for now they say, 'we live in the greatest country in the world'." Jack was stunned because he had always assumed that America meant freedom and liberty.

The saga got even worse. Jack received a call from Lisa a few days later. She was calling from jail. It turned out that Lisa had borrowed a friend's car and had taken off with her kids while visiting them. It was her only chance to get them away from the bad conditions in which they were living in state custody. She was arrested for kidnapping her own children while at the bus station heading for her hometown. Jack could not believe his ears that she was in jail on a criminal charge of kidnapping her own children.

Jack did what he could by taking some money to Dave and Lisa at the jails and visiting with them for moral support. Unfortunately, Jack had to leave town for his work and eventually lost touch with Dave and Lisa.

Jack got to thinking about them. Dave and Lisa had not hurt anyone or done anything that was dangerous to anyone. Dave was in possession of a gun for the protection of his family and a naturally-growing plant. And what did Lisa do wrong? She did not have the money to buy the right state-required paperwork. She was thrown in jail and her kids were taken away, all because of paper. Then she was charged with kidnapping her own kids while attempting to get them back the only way she knew how. "What country do I live in? Nazi Germany?" exclaimed Jack. *(No Jack, you live in Amerika! Land of the fee, home of the slave!)*

> *"Who made thee a prince and a judge over us?"*
> **Exodus 2:14**

This day was a turning point in the way Jack viewed government and all presumed authority over him. Jack asked himself, "Who are these legislative lawmakers and how do they acquire the right to tell me what to do? They are not my master. Have I signed any agreements or contracts that give the government authority over me? How can the government demand my labor against my will if I live in a free country? Does America really stand for freedom, liberty, and justice for all, or is that just what the government wants us to believe? Have I consented and volunteered to be a slave or is the government forcing me into slavery? If I continue to accept this slavery, will my children and grandchildren become enslaved as well? Am I dishonoring the founding fathers of America by allowing government to force me into this slavery and involuntary servitude? Am I doing my country a disservice by accepting all of this?"

It was as though Jack had taken off a blindfold he had been wearing all of his life. Jack realized that injustice was happening to good people on a regular basis at the hands of bad government and presumed legislative authority. For the first time in his life, he was looking at life through the eyes and mind of a totally free individual. He looked back at all of the masters he has had in his life and realized that he unknowingly consented to enslave himself. He realized that maybe, just maybe, he could question authority and good things would happen. It might mean work and hassle but what is the price of true freedom and liberty? Could it be that freedom and liberty are two of our most precious of gifts? Jack had suddenly peeled off all the layers of mind control he had acquired through his life. He had just earned the title of a being a Sovereign Man.

From that day on Jack became a defender of American freedom and liberty. He came to be known as an American Freedom Defender among all who knew him. He knew that he was the only one responsible for asserting and protecting his own personal freedoms and liberties, and that no one would ever do it for him. Further, Jack realized that if he did not assert his God-given rights, allowing the government to enslave him or usurp his rights, he would be part of the problem and would deserve everything that would happen to him. No longer did Jack accept anything at face value from any government entity.

Jack knows now that the way to show loyalty to America is to fight for freedom, liberty, and justice, and to not be fooled or forced to subject his private rights to written statutory jurisdiction. His duty to America is to repair the ills of his government so that it will never create injustice in his witness if he can help it.

It all begins with the protection of every single God-given right, freedom, and liberty. Jack understands that it is wrong to allow any of his rights to be violated for any reason what-so-ever, regardless of what the excuse might be. "If they can force a dollar from me, they can force a thousand. If they can violate one right, they can violate all of my rights." It all became so logical and clear to Jack. He wondered how he could have lived in such a fog all of his life without realizing the simple facts of what real freedom and liberty means.

> *"Wherefore I gave them also statutes whereby they should not live."*
> **Ezekiel 20:25**

Jack did some studying and to his surprise he found that all law-making bodies have only limited authority to regulate government and related consenting commercial activity. No one has the right to force obligations upon the people against their will. This was clearly evident to Jack after reading various writings of our founding fathers. This shocked Jack because all of his adult life he had assumed he was subject to all written laws on the books. What really got to Jack was what he found by merely using his common sense, reading and understanding the Constitution. It was right in front of his face all of his life. He just could not see it. Jack realized that he was not the only one that had been buffaloed. All of society appeared to believe they were subject to legislative law.

Jack came to a stunning revelation. If no written laws pertain to the private rights of people, then people must only believe that these laws pertain to them. People voluntarily consent to the jurisdiction of these written laws by failing to rebut the presumption of law. Jack knew this to be true because he believed the same thing all of his life. It became very clear to him that legislative laws only had jurisdiction over government and related consenting commercial activity, not the private lives of people. Jack wondered how any self-respecting judge could fine and send so many people to jail knowing this fact.

Jack educated himself with the principles of common law, natural law, and the understanding of maxims of law. He read books by John Locke, Thomas Pain, Thomas Jefferson, and other great men of history. Jack now understands that his private life and property are only subject to the authority of God's law, natural law, maxims of law, and the common law of the land, unless he willingly and expressly chooses differently.

One of the most disturbing things Jack found was that the government and every judge he encountered in his fight through the courts, continually attempted to persuade or trick Jack into the delusion that his rights were subject to statute. The courts and government employees continually attempted to defraud Jack with this legal trickery. At times he sat exhausted and at his wits' end from confronting the awesome power and fraud perpetrated by the many departments of government. Jack only knows that if the people of America cannot defeat this clutch of tyranny, that the once-great America will be nothing more than any other tyrannical regime that ever oppressed the people of the world.

Since that day, whenever anyone attempts to assert a claim against Jack, he demands proof of the claim. Any time a government entity attempts to assert the authority of legislative jurisdiction upon him, he comes back with "Who the hell are you and on what document do you rely to make you think I am subject to your legislative jurisdiction?" And sure enough, the government has never proven a statutory claim over Jack. Although Jack took up the fight and spends much of his time fighting government and statutory oppression, he holds the honor of knowing that he is truly a free man and stands firm for the true founding principles of America, freedom, liberty, and justice for all.

> **"Those who expect to reap the blessings of freedom must, like men, undergo the fatigue of supporting it."**
>
> **Thomas Paine**

Let's take a look at Dave and Lisa's situation from the point of statutory law and common law. From the point of statutory law, Dave and Lisa failed to rebut the presumption of law that their private lives were subject to legislative jurisdiction. Therefore, without knowledge of their presumed consent or tacit admission, Dave and Lisa had unknowingly consented to obey all the rules and regulations of legislative jurisdiction. Dave and Lisa failed to obey the written rules and were punished according to the written rule, even though they were not a danger to society and they caused no damage to any other party. Their natural God-given rights and liberties were violated and taken away by the same government whose original intent was to protect those same rights and liberties. Where was the justice?

> **"Justice is incidental to law and order."**
>
> **J. Edgar Hoover**

From the point of common law, natural law, the maxims of law, and God's law, Dave and Lisa were kidnapped, imprisoned, and their children were stolen from them without just cause or due process of law by a government out of control. They were unlawfully sentenced and enslaved by judges who knew that Dave and Lisa's private lives were not subject to legislative authority, which enslaved them, and purposely with malice, denied them due process of law through legal trickery. Dave and Lisa were good family-oriented people who had not caused any damage, infringed upon the rights of anyone, and were certainly not a danger to society. Their family and way of life were destroyed because of words that government employees wrote on paper and called the words laws. Injustice was served by a runaway government which is supposed to protect the rights, liberties, freedoms, and due process of law for the people.

What have we learned from Jack's, Dave's and Lisa's true-life stories? When pertaining to the private rights of the people, true justice in statutory law is very rare, and most of the time statutory law creates serious injustice and violates natural law. Simple common sense will tell us that every situation has to be judged by the facts of the case, always with the consideration of what actual damage or threat has been caused. True justice can never be served by implementing legislative rules and regulations that are presumed to be for the good of the people as a whole. As you can see by what happened to Dave and Lisa, the implementation of statutory law was not for the good of any people at all. Not only did it cause serious psychological effects on Dave and Lisa's children and destroy the way of life for this good young family, it also damaged, to a small degree, that part of the economy that was influenced by Dave and Lisa. That is not to mention the state money wasted on prosecuting and imprisoning Dave and Lisa, foster care for the kidnapped children, the women's shelter, and state assistance. What a mess! Does this make you proud to be an American?

> *"The law isn't justice; It's a very imperfect mechanism. If you press exactly the right buttons and are also lucky, justice may show up in the answer. A mechanism is all the law was ever intended to be."*
> **Raymond Chandler**

More importantly, why do so many people accept the authority of the government over their private lives? As in Jack's case, most people have been conditioned since birth to accept and consent to some form of man made authority. Throughout the lives of most people, different government authorities have stealthily encroached upon people's private lives as they progress from one authority to the next. Because people have been conditioned to believe that questioning authority is usually accompanied by punishment, they consent to authority without question and usually believe they must because "it is the law." It is much the same as training an animal to do more and more tricks. After a while the animal will do any trick without question, because it has been conditioned to do so.

Due to the fact that most people have never been taught about natural law or what true freedom, liberty, and personal sovereignty actually are, they have no point of reference to guide them. Most people are much too busy just living and getting by to contemplate authority, jurisdictions, positive law, maxims of law, due process, common law, or natural law.

Intimidation by government authority plays a big role in the compliance of private individuals to legislative jurisdiction. Not only do private individuals not understand what actual authority legislative law holds, but more often than not private individuals are the ones threatened with punishment for noncompliance with legislative jurisdiction. If they attempt to resist in court, judges will often deny them due process of law for punishment.

Average individuals have no idea that legislative jurisdiction has no authority over their private lives. Again, most people are far too busy and/or ignorant of the common law, natural law, and court procedures to defend themselves against statutory oppression.

> *"To deny the freedom of the will is to make morality impossible."*
>
> **J. A. Froude**

Further, whenever individuals are forced to pay an attorney to defend them in a court action, they are engaged in involuntary servitude since that they have to pay the attorney their hard-earned money for his services to protect the rights that should be respected by the courts in the first place. In other words, punishment begins as soon as they become entangled legally. The government relies on this fact to intimidate citizens into full voluntary compliance.

You have to ask yourself these simple questions: "Will I continue to allow the unscrupulous and ignorant people in control of my American government to continue to ruin America, or will I put forth the effort to challenge these ignorant tyrants and the legislative cancer they have created that is eating away at the fabric of the greatest country in the world, my home?" "If I continue to hide my head in the sand, will this legislative monster go away by itself or will it become so powerful that all of my posterity will be forever doomed to a life of involuntary servitude and slavery?" As you very well know, no one but you will defend your liberties. If you fail to defend your own liberties, you will not only lose your country, you will lose all the rights you failed to defend. This is no joke, it is not an opinion; it is a fact of life.

> *"God grants liberty only to those who love it, and always ready to guard and defend it."*
> **Daniel Webster**

Understanding What and Who
is Behind the Curtain

Pay no attention to that man behind the curtain! yelled the wizard in the movie *The Wizard of Oz*. Was the movie attempting to tell us something in that immortal scene? Similarly, whether by design or by accident (it makes no difference), the government and the judiciary (courts) do not want the people of America to know what is behind their "curtain" of legal deception. It is likely that many people in the government honestly do not know what is going on. It is called compartmentalization.

Compartmentalization is a method of distributing information that prevents one department from knowing what the other departments are doing. Only the management department knows and controls everything in all lower departments.

You will learn what is behind this curtain of deception as you contemplate the subject matter of this book. Let's take a good look at how the government tricks you into believing what you think you know. First we must understand some basics.

There are two basic types of law that are distinctly different from each other. The first is natural law which is called common law, "the law of the people," or simply "the law." The law relies on all the established maxims of law and principles developed and accepted throughout history, and are the root of all written and unwritten law. We will learn these principles later in this book.

The other type of law is legislative law, which consists of all written laws and statutes. Written law is also called positive law, enacted law, statutory law, admiralty law, maritime law, codes, regulations, etc. Legislative law is enacted by law making bodies such as Congress, the legislature or state and local law making bodies. It is extremely important to understand that legislative law holds authority and jurisdiction **only** over government entities and related consenting commerce, such as the military, corporations and licensed entities, etc.

The people who comprise the Congress, legislature or any other law making bodies were never given any type of awesome, kingly power to rule the private lives of people. It is the legislators' job description to create rules and laws for the management and proper development of government and relating consenting commerce. There is no lawful or moral duty of any citizen to forfeit any rights or liberties due to the enactment of any legislative law. The only reason this absurd myth ever got started was due to the people's inability to understand the basics of the law of the people and what their rights really are. Basically someone said it was the law and the people blindly said OK.

According to common law and the founding principles and documents of America, legislative law holds no authority or jurisdiction over the private lives of people without their consent. Law-making bodies hold no authority to make laws that pertain to private individuals' lives, properties, and affairs. If they did, it would make all lawmaking bodies the king and master of the people, effectively nullifying the people's freedoms and liberties. This was not the intent of our founding fathers, founding documents, the American government or our way of life. We will explore how this "consent" is presumed by governments later in this book. In a nut shell there is no documentation that gives any government employee or lawmaker any authority over the inherent unalienable rights of the people.

> *"What light is to the eye, what air is to the lungs, what love is to the heart, liberty is to the soul of man."*
> **R. G. Ingersoll**

Natural law, "the law," or common law is the unwritten law of the land that is determined by common sense, logical deduction, the maxims of law, and the rational reasoning of man. The maxims of law are listed later in this book.

The principles of natural law pertain to all people and entities, with or without their consent. Natural law is the law that governed mankind long before written enacted positive law ever came into existence. Essentially, the primary law of man and society is this: **You cannot create damage, infringe upon the rights of others or create an obvious danger.** All societies could be ruled by this all-encompassing law, the root of all law. All written law must comply with this all encompassing law. It is the law.

Natural law is also called common law since it is based on common sense and maxims of law, and is the law of the common people. You might say that common law is the format in which natural law is expressed and presented into the courts. Common law is the foundation of all written positive laws.

A legislative positive law cannot lawfully violate common law. By our system of laws in America as it was originally intended, any positive law (written legislative law) that violates natural law is void.

This is reflected in positive law as well as Supreme Court decisions:

> Where rights secured by the Constitution are involved, there can be no rule-making or legislation which would abrogate them.
> (Key No. 73, <u>Miranda *vs* State of Arizona</u>, 86 S. Ct. 1602 [1966])

> An unconstitutional statute, though having the form and name of law, is in reality no law, but is wholly null and void and ineffective for any purpose.
> It imposes no duty, confers no rights, creates no office, bestows no power or authority on anyone, affords no protection and justifies no acts performed under it. No one is bound to obey an unconstitutional statute and no courts are bound to enforce it. (16 <u>Am. Jur.</u>, 2nd Sec. 177)

> Law repugnant to the Constitution is void. (U.S. Sup. Ct., <u>*Marbury vs. Madison*</u>, 1803, L.Ed. 60: Cra. 137: of 6 Whea: 246 & Wal 601)

As you can readily see, all legislative law must have a lawful basis in the founding principles of common law, which abides by all maxims of law. If they did not, then they would obviously violate "the law." That is just pure common sense and logic.

The Constitution was basically the first positive law enacted by our government that protected common law from being violated by the government.

Two elements must exist before it can be considered that a violation of the common law has been committed. There must first be some form of actual damage or infringement upon another's liberties, or a clear and obvious danger (such as bringing a suitcase full of explosives into a movie theater). In other words, a jury would determine the Defendant as being obviously dangerous and negligent as to put others in serious danger.

Secondly, there must be someone willing to swear under oath they know of the damage or danger, and know or believe by evidence that the Defendant has created the damage or danger. Only then can an indictment against the perpetrator be served lawfully. This requirement is protected by the fourth amendment of the Bill of Rights to the Constitution. Our forefathers knew very well how the king's court could make purely arbitrary decisions and violate the rights of people at will. Our forefathers wrote the Constitution to control the government. The Constitution has nothing to do with the rights of the people other than to protect their inherent unalienable rights. Learn the Constitution and the Bill of Rights. It is important to understand these founding documents.

The Constitution is a contract that tells government how to operate and how to respect the rights of the people in compliance with the common law of the land. The Constitution is supposed to keep our government from turning into a king or dictator. But legal trickery, ignorance, and erroneous beliefs have side-stepped the authority of the Constitution. The primary cause is that private individuals have lost the ability to exercise the authority of the Constitution over the government.

Remember this one all-important fact: The people were born with inherent unalienable right and liberties. They did not get their rights from the Constitution. The Constitution merely guarantees that your natural rights will not be violated by the government. The

Constitution is the law that governs the government, not the people. Common law governs the people.

Now that you understand the difference between legislative law and common law (natural law), we can move onto the next very important subject.

> *"Free government is founded in jealousy and not in confidence; it is jealousy and not confidence which prescribes limited Constitutions to bind down those whom we are obliged to trust with power. In questions of power then let not more heard of confidence in man, but bind him down from mischief by the chains of the Constitution."*
> **Thomas Jefferson**

The most important thing to realize is that lawmaking bodies in America only have authority to make laws, rules, and regulations that pertain to the operation and management of government and consenting commercial activities and entities (i.e. trade). *This truth must never be forgotten and must be understood by all people!*

If you forget this truth, you are forgetting the truth of freedom and liberty and you are no better than a slave. The government wants you to believe that your private rights are subject to legislative enactment. This is the crux and main tool of their fraud.

Yes, it is true that you really don't have a master and you really don't have to answer to anyone except who you choose to answer to.

Sure, if you are working for government, then part or all of your profession may be guided by positive law. You must have a clear distinction between private life, which is dictated by common law, and commercial activity, that is dictated by positive law. These are very simple concepts to differentiate. The more you ponder these concepts the clearer they become. Think about the concept of being totally free before you go to sleep or upon waking up. Achieving a sovereign mentality may take a little work at first, but once you recognize and shake off the past mind control, you will never go back to thinking like a slave. When your first glimpse of your new sovereign mentality emerges, it is a ray of sunshine and a fresh breath of air.

The sole purpose of our founding fathers' creation of our American form of government was to regulate government to promote trade, to protect our borders from aggression, and to secure the blessings of liberty for ourselves and our posterity.

There are *no* lawmaking bodies in America that have any authority to make laws, rules, or regulations that can be forced upon any free individual in America absent his consent.

Get this one all important fact into your head and never forget it. No documentation exists that would prove otherwise.

This is the fraud that allows government to usurp the rights of the people. The government can only operate their fraud upon the people when the people believe that their rights, freedoms, and liberties can be controlled by the legislature.

Our American form of government was created to specifically forbid any kind of ruler or king over the free people. The people rule themselves by the guidelines of the common law in their day-to-day lives.

American government is operated by consent. The offices and positions of president, Congress, Senate, legislatures, and the like, were created only to run the government and have nothing to do with the private lives of the free people. Only the common law has rightful jurisdiction over the private people.

"That government is best which governs the least, because its people discipline themselves."

Thomas Jefferson

What is not taught in school and has been long forgotten and neglected is the fact that all free people of America are free sovereign individuals with no rulers over their private lives or property. All people of America are subject only to the rules of common law. The common law is based on all maxims of law, common sense, and logical reason.

Of course, people can knowingly and freely volunteer to become subject to a legislative jurisdiction if they so desire. People may be involved in a business or license that is engaging with government and governed by statute. An individual may also lose his freedom and become subject to a legislative jurisdiction because he may have been convicted of a crime, and has become a prisoner. He has now lost his freedom and is subject to the will of the legislative penal system.

The free people of America are able to do anything they desire, so long as they do not create damage, create an obvious danger, or infringe upon the liberties of others. This is the original intent and design of the American government created by our founding fathers. This is specifically why America seceded from England's rule. Because of this free and uninhibited mentality of the people, America became the strongest and most productive nation in the world. This is the American way.

> *"Rightful liberty is unobstructed action according to our will within limits drawn around us by the equal rights of others. I do not add within the limits of the law because law is often but the tyrant's will, and always so when it violates the rights of the individual."*
> **Thomas Jefferson**

Does this fact shock you? Do you think Thomas Jefferson is wrong? Your logic and common sense tells you that you have always known this, although you may have never had the chance to fully realize it. If you do not believe the aforementioned facts, stop right now and attempt to prove them wrong. I can assure you that you cannot dispel any of these facts.

If you cannot see the logic in this, then maybe you are not suited to be a free individual. Or possibly you are employed by the government and you feel your paycheck will suffer if you think out of your box of denial. And you have the perfect right to be guided in your private life by a master if you so choose. If you chose to make the government your master, this is your God-given right.

You can freely waive your freedoms and liberties at any time by merely giving your consent. Just as you do when you go to work for an employer or join the military. While you are at work you waive many of your freedoms and liberties because you are receiving compensation from your employer. But never forget for a minute that you can force others against their will to do the same. If you had the right and power to force obligations upon others against their will, you would be no better than any unjust ruler, dictator, or king that ever created injustice upon this earth.

If any person, lawmaking body, or government could force you to do their bidding or force you into some form of involuntary servitude, then of course they would be acting in a capacity of being your master, ruler, or tyrant. You would be subservient to such authority and you would be no different from a subject, serf, or slave, regardless of how you might fool yourself into believing otherwise. No matter how many times you might say you have freedom and liberty, it would be a lie of denial every time you said it.

Living in America and believing that you are free does not take away from the fact that, if you are forced to perform or pay, you are engaged in the involuntary servitude that is prohibited by maxims of law and the Thirteenth Amendment to the Constitution.

Remember, your money is a note. It is a tool for exchanging value that reflects your labor or servitude. When you are forced to give up your "tool for exchanging value," then you are forced into involuntary servitude. You are forced to supply your labor for free because someone else has taken the benefit of your work from you. It violates your rights and the law.

It does not matter if you are under some form of mind control, believing it is only taxes. Facts are facts. If you are forced to pay taxes, you are engaged in involuntary servitude, just as any slave or serf ever was.

Let's look at it this way. Everything government does has to be documented. What documentation or contract does any lawmaking body have that gives them authority over your personal life without your consent?

There is none, period. Case closed! If you believe otherwise, you owe it to yourself to investigate this all-important fact. You can look for this documentation until hell freezes over. What this means is that all written legislative laws, rules, regulations, etc., have absolutely no lawful mandatory effect upon your private life unless you willingly volunteer or consent to abide by such laws, or rules.

This is why the IRS says that paying income tax is by voluntary compliance. The people are only subject to the rule of common law.

> *"One man with courage makes a majority."*
> **Andrew Jackson**

Yes, you may submit or volunteer your private life or properties into legislative authority if you so desire. You may do this by simply failing to rebut any presumed jurisdiction that attempts to force you to comply. In other words, you have the right to challenge or not challenge any jurisdiction. By law, any time a jurisdiction is challenged, the government must prove such jurisdiction.

And on the reverse side, if you fail to rebut the presumption that a positive law pertains to you, then by the rule of law you have agreed to be subject to the positive law, by merely remaining silent and by not contesting the forced obligation or authority.

In other words, suppose I sued you and claimed that you owed me $1000. Of course, you have the right to make me prove why I believe that you owe me the $1000. This is simple common sense according to natural law. But if you failed to challenge my claim, then by law you must owe it to me because you failed to challenge my claim. This is called "operation of law." If I assert a claim against you and you fail to rebut the claim, then by operation of law, you have admitted by your silence in the matter, that my claim is valid. This is called your "tacit admission," meaning your admission by remaining silent on the matter. This is one of the most basic foundations of law. Without this simple process, law could not operate properly and people could not effectively assert their truths in courts of law.

Think of it this way: In your day-to-day life, does anyone ever force obligations upon you? No, and if they did, there would be an instant conflict. It never happens on a normal basis. What this proves is that all forced obligations are an injustice and causes conflict.

People naturally protest if someone forces an obligation upon them. But most people never say a word when their "lord and master" forces the obligation. They may get punished for such insolence! Besides, it is much easier to believe the myth that the government would cease to function if it did not force everyone to do their "fair share." At least it makes the victim feel better about being forced into involuntary servitude.

It is important to understand the difference between the words "legal" and "lawful." "Legal" pertains to all matters of positive written law. "Lawful" pertains to all matters of common law or natural law, which has its basis in maxims of law. In other words, it is illegal to drive your car without license plates, but it is not unlawful. It is generally unlawful to steal something. But sometimes it can be legal by some form of legislative law that creates injustice, such as stealing an individual's home for the non-payment of property tax. Driving without plates violates a written legislative law, but no common law has been broken. If you steal something you have broken a maxim of law or common law, regardless whether there is a written law that pertains to the act.

There are some things that may be completely lawful to do, but may be illegal. For example, it would be completely lawful to have a controlled and safe campfire on a beach where there was no damage or nuisance caused. But it may be illegal because there are regulations that do not permit campfires on that particular beach.

> *"Experience should teach us to be most on our guard to protect liberty when the government's purposes are beneficial. The greatest dangers to liberty lurk in insidious encroachment by men of zeal, well meaning but without understanding."*
> **Louis D. Brandeis**

Let's look at how the judiciary and government perceive the meaning of words that many of us take for granted with completely different meanings.

Many words that you use in common language may have a completely different legal definition. Legal definitions are those that are used by courts of law, judges, attorneys, corporations, public entities, and the like.

Let's look at a common example. Most people think that the word "citizen" means simply an individual that lives in a certain state or country. You may find it surprising what the legal definition of "citizen" really is. The following definitions are all definitions in part or in whole from *Black's Law Dictionary,* sixth edition.

It is extremely important that you read the definitions carefully and understand what each word means from a legal perspective. I will assist you, but you must read everything very carefully with full comprehension. Pay particular attention to the underlined phrases and highlighted words. *All the words set in bold are key definitions that are defined further below.*

All italicized words and phrases must be understood from the legal definition.

Citizen: One who, <u>*under the Constitution and laws*</u> of the United States, or of a particular state, is a <u>*member of the political community*</u>, owing **allegiance** and being <u>*entitled*</u> to the enjoyment of full civil rights. All **persons** born or naturalized in the United States <u>*and subject to the jurisdiction*</u> thereof are citizens of the United States and the state wherein they reside.

Citizens are members of a political community who, in their associated capacity, have established or **submitted** themselves to the **dominion** of a government for the promotion of their general welfare and the protection of their individual as well as <u>*collective rights*</u>.

Notice that the first line says under the Constitution and the laws of the United States. This means one who is subject to the written legislative enactments created by lawmakers. Remember that the government and its employees are the only ones subject to the written laws and the Constitution.

The Constitution is a lawful guideline for the government to follow, not for the people to follow. The people are subject only to the primary law, which says that you cannot create damage, infringement upon the rights of others, an obvious danger to others.

If you are a *member of the political community*, you are probably engaged in some form of government activity. If you are working for the government you owe allegiance to your employer. Your employer pays you to owe allegiance. Civil rights are rights granted to you by a government. Civil rights are not to be confused with natural rights with which you are endowed by your creator.

All persons that are *subject* to the jurisdiction thereof are citizens. Are you subject to the jurisdiction of legislative law? And if so, how do you know? Are you subject to these written words merely because someone wrote them down?

Read the legal definition of "person" below and realize that when the judiciary says person, they mean a legal entity and not a natural human being.

Further the definition of citizen states: <u>"Members of a political community (government) that have submitted to the dominion of a government."</u> In other words, the legal community considers that you have waived your natural rights and have become subservient to a government by becoming a citizen.

> *"We must remember that a right lost to one, is lost to all."*
> **William Reece Smith Jr.**

Now carefully read all of the definitions from *Black's Law Dictionary* of the words from the definition of citizen above, that are set in bold type.

Allegiance: **Obligation** of **fidelity** and **obedience** to government in consideration for protection that government gives.

Person: In general usage (common language), a human being (i.e., natural person). By *statute term* (legally) may include labor organizations, partnerships, associations, corporations, legal representatives, trustees, trustees in bankruptcy, or receivers.

Submitted: To **commit** to the discretion of another. To yield *to the will* of another.

Dominion: *Perfect control in right of ownership*. The word implies both title and possession and appears to require a <u>complete retention of control</u> over disposition. **Title** (see definition below) to an article of property which arises from the power of disposition and the right of claiming it.

Title: The formal right of ownership of property.

Obligation: That which a person is bound to do or forbear; any duty imposed by law, promise, contract, relations of society, courtesy, kindness, etc.

Obedience: Compliance with a command, prohibition, or known law of rule of duty prescribed.

Fidelity: Continuing faithfulness to a person, cause, or belief.

Commit: To entrust; to pledge.

Subject: One that owes allegiance to a sovereign and is governed by his laws. The natives of Great Britain are subjects of the British government. **Men in free governments are subjects as well as citizens.** As citizens they enjoy rights and franchises; as subjects they are bound to obey the laws. The term is rarely used in this sense in countries enjoying a republican form of government.

Remember: All of the above definitions are straight from *Black's Law Dictionary*, 6th edition.

Would you take offense if you were held obligated to the legal definition of citizen?

What does this all mean? It means that the government and the courts take silent judicial notice (they presume) that all citizens have submitted their private lives, affairs, and property to the dominion of the sovereign government and that they are obligated to abide by, and be obedient to, all written legislative laws. This is very similar to the treatment of military personnel, serfs, and slaves.

Although in reality this could be construed as fraud because the unsuspecting citizen is unaware of what is happening, the legal community can get away with it because the citizen has not done his due diligence to become informed properly. Now you are informed!

> *"A little neglect may breed great mischief. . . for want of a nail the shoe was lost; for want of a shoe the horse was lost; and for want of a horse the rider was lost."*
> **Benjamin Franklin**

Did you ever imagine that neglecting to understand the meaning of citizen could subject you to so much hidden obligations? It would not set well with most folks to be called subjects or slaves, so the government uses the word citizen. Citizen just sounds so much nicer than slave.

Although I say this in a most joking manner, I can assure you that it is of one of the most important issues of our time. This one presumption of law is the way that every tyrannical government or ruler since the beginning of time has imposed its will upon the people. It is the crux, keystone, and linchpin of the entire fraud upon the people and freedom. *It causes the people to generally accept that the government has the right to violate their rights for the common good.* This erroneous concept has been repeated time and time again throughout history. It is time that a procedure is created in which all can rely on maxims of law for the protection of rights and liberties. The original system of law needs to be re-instituted in which common sense, the facts, and maxims of law are held paramount, not the legislature. By law, no individual or government has the right to violate maxims of law.

Now that you have a pretty good background about what this book is going to address, let's get into the nitty-gritty and find out just how this whole fraud against the people of the world and America came about.

> *"Man is free at the moment he wishes to be."*
> **Voltaire**

Governments

It has long been a common misconception, to confuse society with government. Society is produced by the wants of the people. Government has generally been formed to regulate and protect the commerce of society. As society could exist without government using natural law as its guide, government could not exist without society. And without society, government would hold no purpose. In the purest form, one might conclude that people create society and society creates government.

Another general misconception is the distinction between governing and ruling. Governing can be described as handling the affairs of government for the promotion and general well-being of the society, whereas ruling is the dictating of conduct and domination of the private lives of the inhabitants of the society. A just government may govern the commerce of a society, whereas a dictator, king, or emperor will rule and dominate the people by dictating what they can and cannot do in their private lives and possessions.

> *"The power to tax involves the power to destroy."*
> **John Marshall**

As history has shown us, many people of this world have descended from generations who have been dominated and ruled. This is how most societies have been ruled since the beginning of time. Most often it was the strongest that ruled, not the fairest or most benevolent. This was most often the case as the strongest and most ruthless would most often prevail in a primitive world. The mind set of the members of most societies is such that they cannot imagine true freedom, independence, or liberty, primarily because they have never truly experienced it. They instinctively expect to be told what to do and when and where to do it. It is ingrained so deeply in the minds of men that they instinctively ask for permission or ask themselves whether or not they are allowed to do anything before they do it. For the sake of discussion, we will call people with this "ruled" mentality "serfs, subjects, or slaves." We will refrain from using the word citizen so we do not hurt the feelings of those citizens who may still be in denial.

A free, sovereign individual has no ruler or master besides his creator. A free, honest, and sane man in a state of nature instinctively understands natural law and knows right from wrong. He knows when he is causing damage or when he is causing an obvious danger to others. This sovereign individual in a state of nature needs no set of written rules by which to abide. A free man instinctively understands natural law by way of reason, and knows when he is doing wrong. He is ruled by his conscience, common sense and reason. A truly free man knows that he may exercise his freedoms and liberties any way he wishes, as long as his exercise does not create damage, an obvious danger, or infringement upon the liberties of others. This is generally termed as living within the common law of the land or natural law.

Throughout the ages, most people of the world have been ruled by masters, kings, emperors, dictators, strongmen, and the like. You might say that it was just part of the evolution of human civilization. Throughout history, ruling governments more often than not, evolved into oppression of its people in one form or another, as ruling itself is a form of oppression. It has always been the way of man and nature for the strong to dominate the weak.

> *"When one by force subdues men, they do not submit to him in heart. They submit because their strength is not adequate to resist."*
>
> **Mencius**

In the days of old if a king wanted more taxes, more men for the military, one's wife or daughter, one's land or life, there was nothing to be done against the awesome power of the king. There was no one to turn to for protection. There was no 911, no world court. No one was more powerful than the king. Of course, under these conditions, even if it were a benevolent king, you would be convinced by force and intimidation that your contribution was for the good of the kingdom.

And so the classes of royalty remained royal and the classes of subjects, serfs, and slaves remained forever locked into involuntary servitude from generation to generation. Of course, in a benevolent kingdom the serfs believe their lives were good. And in fact many serfs did live good lives, compared to the alternative of some other tyrannical rulers. Their involuntary servitude was a small price to pay when considering the alternative: leaving your home, family and friends to live under another ruler who might be less benevolent.

Many people do very well being dominated, especially when there is no other alternative. The mentality of personal sovereignty, true freedom, and liberty has been so far removed from the conscience of men that they accept feudalism as a way of normal life. Throughout the centuries fear and intimidation have been major factors in the evolution of civilization and societies. Just ask anyone why they pay their income taxes and they will tell you, "Well, if we don't, they will take our possessions and throw us in jail. It's the law, you know!"

This is not to say that there were not a number of truly benevolent societies that respected the rights and liberties of all of their inhabitants. Of course there must have been some societies that truly governed by reason and natural law. It is a sad state of affairs that many of these successful societies were overtaken by barbarian strongmen. Until the age of technology one's survival depended upon how well the warriors of the society could swing a sword or shoot an arrow. No matter how great the society, if it failed to provide a formidable defense, it would surely be overtaken by foreign warriors, whose sole existence was predicated on violating the rights and liberties of other people for their own personal gain.

> *"Liberties and masters are not easily combined."*
> **Tacitus**

These benevolent societies would have flourished if not for the heavy hand of men bent on domination, destruction, and control. The capture of a benevolent society was devastating to its inhabitants. It destroyed their cultures, sciences, and goodness. The men were killed or enslaved and the woman, children, and property, were left at their mercy. And one must remind oneself that the dominated people became the second class and oppressed people of the ruling society. As a rule, they became slaves with no rights or liberties for long periods of time. The brilliance, the culture, the innocence lost, all because might prevailed over good, reason, natural law, and the laws of just societies.

The air of oppression in a society is overwhelmingly contrary to the promotion of a free society. The amount of oppression is in direct proportion to the degradation of freedom and liberty of the people of any society. So as you could easily imagine, the mind set of civilization had as much chance of going forward as of going backward. The chance of freedom and liberty flourishing was completely dependent on the ability to defeat an attacking enemy. The victor was not always a benevolent one. And to make things even worse, the warrior defenders of a society often became the oppressive masters of the society they defended.

> *"Government is not reason, it is not eloquence, it is force; like fire, a troublesome servant and a fearful master. Never for a moment should it be left to irresponsible action."*
> **George Washington**

Examining these particular scenarios of evolution, it is clearly evident that the master and slave mentality is deeply rooted in the psyche of man. A man will capitulate to almost anything if he is forced to. Hunger, despair, and the need to protect one's family will cause anyone to do almost anything. People learn to cope with adverse situations and in the process cover up their free-spirit mentality. The absence of this free spirit-mentality in turn causes them to forget the principles of natural law, true freedom, and liberty. Throughout the evolution of man and society the maxim has always been, "do with what you have and survive." As life is, you take the cards you are dealt. Many of us have never lived without power, phones, refrigerators, running water, stores close by, motorized vehicles. In the days of old you ate what was produced within a ten-mile radius. In the non-growing seasons, you ate what you had saved and stored. You could imagine being hungry during a drought or long freeze and suddenly you may have to deal with a foreign army on its way to do you harm.

During the centuries of evolution, man has been kept from evolving to a higher state of being by the oppression by those more powerful and forceful. The more freedom and liberty the people of a society have, the more benevolent and prosperous they become. If no one is oppressed in the society, it helps all of society. This is why America became so successful in the beginning years. All American's had more freedoms and liberty than citizens of any other country in the world.

As we have just examined, it is not hard to understand how whole races and countries of people could be forced out of their natural understanding of true freedom and liberty. Their survival itself depended upon their capitulation to the dominating force or authority.

> *"A little rebellion . . . is a medicine necessary for the sound health of government."*
> **Thomas Jefferson**

Dogs, Wolves and Men

L et's examine the similarities between the mentality of a serf/ slave and a domesticated dog, and the similarities between the mentality of a free man and a wolf in the wild.

It is common knowledge that a wolf is considerably harder to train and domesticate than a domesticated dog. If one were to capture an adult wild wolf and attempt to train him, it would be nearly impossible to truly domesticate the wolf. Many times these caged animals will simply die in captivity. It has been said by many who have tried that even at best you can never really domesticate a wolf that has once run free. If this same captive wolf were to be set free again in the wild, he would revert to his free state of mind and being.

Similar to the wolf, a truly free man that has lived free for some time is resistant to accepting any form of slavery, serfdom, feudalism, forced obligations, or authority over him. Like the wolf, once an individual has tasted true freedom, he cannot be caged without the urge to forever try to escape to freedom once more.

The domesticated dog has come from an ancestry of domesticated dogs. The domesticated breeds are much easier to train and control than the wild wolf. Over generations of breeding, it is well established in the genetic makeup of the dog to readily accept domestication. The dog is usually said to be loyal, faithful, and obedient to his master's commands, even in the face of abuse and punishment. This domestication has been bred into the dog for generations upon generations.

A cruel master can easily abuse the domesticated dog and the dog will cower, take the abuse, but most often remain loyal. But I dare say that anyone abusing a wild wolf would expect nothing but a vicious, angry attack.

Similar to the domesticated dog, a slave, serf, subject, or individual that has lived a life of involuntary servitude under the command of another, would find his situation commonplace and normal. The serf would most often find that when he pleased his master good things would happen to his situation and living conditions. Conversely, when he displeased his master bad things would happen and punishment would ensue. Is this starting to sound familiar?

> *"Few men desire liberty; most men wish only for a just master."*
> **Sallust**

It would be quite normal for the serf to teach his children the ways of a good and obedient serf because in his eyes he loves his children and wants only good things to happen to them. It would become normal for the serf to even believe he has freedom, even if he only had a small amount of freedom for himself. It would become second nature to do whatever might please his master without question. It would be well known by all of the serfs that the master would disapprove and punish all those who even thought of questioning his authority or forced obligations.

So consequently it would become a taboo subject among all the serfs to engage in any activity that the master might disapprove of. It would even be found that some serfs would turn against other serfs that might contemplate actions against the master. The rebelling serf would be labeled traitorous and be condemned by the other serfs. Besides, the serfs would have lived for generations in many different forms of involuntary servitude and would have never known or tasted true freedom. The serf's point of view would be from only slavery and serfdom. It would be the same as a man that has always been blind in one eye all of his life. He cannot possibly know what it would be like to see with both eyes because he has never experienced it.

It is the nature of most living things to be free. If you take any individual or animal and put it in a cage and treat it poorly, it will want to flee the cage. Freedom is a natural instinct to most species.

Many wild species of animals simply die when placed in captivity. I would challenge anyone to contradict this maxim of logical thought.

But what about caging an individual or animal and treating it well. It may come to rely on its regular good treatment and become used to its cage. Such individuals in prison have no desire to leave because they have become institutionalized. But start treating these prisoners or caged animals poorly again and you will see them all with the desire to flee the cage. Any that would stay under adverse conditions would truly be in a pitiful state of being.

Are the citizens of America being treated well by their master? They have cars, homes, schools, and TVs. When they are not working they can come and go when they want, and have the illusion of true freedom. And they are certainly better off than those in some other countries. They only have to work part of the year for their master and they get to keep part of the money they earn. They have the illusion of owning their own home and their master will only kick them out if they fail to pay the master's rent which he calls income tax and property tax. The citizens are treated so well by their master that they really don't want to leave their cage. You might say that the people of America live in the best cell in the prison. Besides, the master tells them that they live in the freest country in the world and that they must forfeit some of their natural rights or the country will fall into anarchy. Then there will be no more schools or paved roads. The citizens are very content because they usually have enough money to buy all the freedom they need. Besides, they know that they will be punished if they do not comply willingly. What about the people that do not have enough money? They have insufficient resources to effectively complain, so they just become wallpaper in the house of pain. Nobody really notices or even cares.

> *"There is no injury which is done with (the injured one's) consent."*
>
> **Ulpianus**

Freedom in the true sense of the word can be defined as free will achieved by using conscience, common sense, natural law, and

God as a guide. True freedom has no master or ruling authority other than the creator. A truly free man who exercises true freedom, chooses what authorities and obligations, if any, he may subject his life to, such as his job, marriage, church, government, and so on. He has a natural right to own his home and possessions without fear of having them taken away. A man ceases to be free when he no longer has a choice of his free will or obligations. If a man is forced to perform against his will, he is engaged in involuntary servitude and is in one form or another, a slave.

It does not matter whether the obligation is a little or a lot. The point is that an obligation is being forced. If the government can force a dollar from someone, then they can force a thousand. At what point does a man cease to be free? One dollar? Ten dollars? One hundred dollars? The correct answer is "anytime an obligation is forced upon him, regardless of how small."

> *"There is a point beyond which even justice becomes unjust."*
> **Sophocles**

People, who live under the rule of a king, emperor, dictator, or the like, are not free and have no choice in the matter. Many times these people are told by their ruler that they are free, and many believe it as well. The masses will believe most anything. During World War II, the people of Japan believed their emperor was a god. They had an authority who controlled their lives and they accepted it. Resistance to this authority usually ended in punishment of some sort.

We can very well see how people can become used to their environments even to the point where misery and involuntary servitude become normal and commonplace.

Kings and Kingdoms

L et us examine some different scenarios about how kings become kings. Let us examine how a typical kingdom might have come into being centuries ago. We will assume for the sake of discussion that this kingdom was not taken by force (or conquered), and evolved naturally.

Generally a ruler of the people gained power by force or simply by becoming the richest in the land. Today we have commercial laws that prohibit monopolies and business practices such as "dumping." "Dumping" is the practice of producing something and selling it at a loss in order to drive your competition out of business. One can very easily visualize a situation wherein a very rich individual could monopolize the commerce of a small area and eventually end up owning all property. It is obvious that a very rich man can have total financial control over an area inhabited by people of modest means.

Suppose a very rich man in a village decided that he wanted the land that belonged to a saddle maker. The rich man would have simply hired other saddle makers to produce saddles for him. The rich man can afforded to lose money on the sale of his saddles, and would sell the saddles at such a low price that the saddle maker could not make a living. The saddle maker would go broke and be forced to sell his land to the rich man or his agent.

> *"When the well's dry, we know the worth of water."*
> **Benjamin Franklin**

This process could go on and on until the rich man owned all property and businesses in his area. In that case anyone who wished to live on the rich man's land would have had to work for, and answer to the rich man, who by this time would have been called a king. The king would have eventually had all the people that lived on his land in his hire and he would be receiving portions of their crops or trade for rent or taxes.

The king, for the protection of his kingdom would naturally have had to hire and train men to protect and carry out duties relating to the preservation of his kingdom. These men would have been called soldiers and would have comprised the king's army.

After generations had past, the people of the kingdom would have grown accustomed to feudalism and to being ruled by the king. They would have known no other type of life and would have had no other place to go, besides another kingdom. Consequently the fate of the people was strictly dictated by the whim of whatever king happened to inherit the throne.

> **"Truth forever on the scaffold, Wrong forever on the throne."**
> **James Russell Lowell**

This above example is typical of how a rich man could easily come to rule and dominate the lives of many people. He would become king because he was shrewd in business, not necessarily because he was a good or deserving man.

It is not hard to understand that the best interests of the people were generally not the main concern of the king. With the king in complete control of all affairs, his own best interests and those of his kingdom would be his primary concerns.

Although kings and kingdoms evolved in a multitude of ways, the result was the same. The people who lived in the kingdoms were subject to involuntary servitude and control.

So, just as dogs evolved into domestication, so most people of the world evolved into the slave mentality, through generation after generation. The slave mentality becomes so ingrained that it becomes second nature for people to never question their ruler (that is, their king, emperor, dictator, president, chief).

The New World

So it came to pass that most of the people of Europe were oppressed by their rulers in one form or another. There were no real free societies. The conditions were so bad that the thought of risking one's life in a wooden ship sailing across the Atlantic to a wild and unforgiving land seemed attractive.

> *"O! Ye that love mankind! Ye that dare oppose not only the tyranny but the tyrant, stand forth! Every spot of the Old World is overrun with oppression. Freedom hath been hunted round the globe. Asia and Africa have long expelled her. Europe regards her like a stranger and England hath given her warning to depart. O! Receive the fugitive and prepare in time an asylum for mankind."*
>
> **Thomas Paine**

Once these "subjects" arrived in this new world, they found life entirely different from that of their homeland. They found that they had to band together as a society of mutual interest for survival. Although England was in control of America, there was very little governmental control, as England was half a world away, across a vast ocean. There were no written laws to speak of. The people governed themselves by natural law. All men of honest reflection and common sense were certainly able to ascertain right from wrong and determine when damage was being done. They needed no authority to guide their conscience. The people were not being oppressed and found that, although symbolically they were still British subjects, there was no everyday evidence of being ruled. It was their first taste of true freedom. This is something that very few, if any, had ever experienced.

After a generation or two had gone by, something very interesting started to emerge. The people of America began to lose their "serf/subject/slave" mentality. The people began to wonder why they were obligated to a king in a foreign land. Most of the people by this time had been born in America and had only heard about a place called England. Most of the people really did not fully understand the concept of a ruler or king. The concept of a ruling king was something that most Americans had only talked or read about. Actual evidence of a ruling king was never experienced by the Americans until English soldiers began enforcing the king's authority and obligations upon them.

The people of America were beginning to think like free people, guided by conscience, common sense and natural law. The thought of having to ask permission or pay homage to a king was not in them.

The king realized that his subjects in America were printing their own money and were beginning to slip from his control. This was certainly not to be tolerated. The king began to institute more and more taxes and tariffs on the trade of America. He forbade his American subjects from printing their own money. The king's soldiers were instituting more and more obligations upon the people. Many people of America began to resist as they realized that being under the control of England was a hindrance to the prosperity of the people and their continent. They did not take lightly their personal liberties being under attack.

> *"Let us contemplate our forefathers, and posterity, and resolve to maintain the rights bequeathed to us from the former, for the sake of the latter. The necessity of the times, more than ever, calls for our utmost circumspection, deliberation, fortitude, and perseverance. Let us remember that 'if we suffer tamely a lawless attack upon our liberty, we encourage it, and involve others in our doom.' It is a very serous consideration. . . that millions yet unborn may be the miserable sharers of the event."*
> **Samuel Adams**

There were many people, though, who could not shake their subject mentality. Many people of America wanted to stay under the king's rule as they were receiving some form of benefit from England. Some were just plain afraid of the consequences, in much the same way as people feel today if they resist the forced obligations of the American government. These people were called loyalists. Many loyalists at that time called supporters of the revolution "traitors." The men called "traitors" are what Americans call forefathers or the founding fathers of America.

When the Revolutionary War broke out, many of the loyalists were apprehensive about what to do. If they stayed loyal to the king and England lost the war, they would be considered traitors in their own land. If they sided with the revolutionists and England won, they would be branded as traitors as well.

The revolutionists on the other hand knew that there was nothing more important than their freedoms and liberties. They risked their homes, businesses, families, and their lives for the cause of freedom. The serf mentality was gone from their conscience. Like wolves in the wild, they were never to return to captivity. These honorable men and women risked all to form one of the greatest experiments in government that the world has ever known. Never before had an entire continent endeavored to create a government in which all of its inhabitants were free sovereign people. All free men and women in America were to be their own kings. They were kings of their own properties and lives. "It's good to be King!"

> *"Let us therefore animate and encourage each other, and show the whole world that a Freeman, contending for liberty on his own ground, is superior to any slavish mercenary on earth."*
> **George Washington**

So it came to pass that America formed its own government. The purpose of American government was not to rule the people as a king. The purpose of America's government was to regulate its commerce and foreign trade, to protect its borders from invaders, and to ensure that the people could rely on the common law of the land for their personal protection and lawful activities. They financed the government through commerce with tariffs and trade and never imposed obligations upon the private rights of the people.

It was a matter of common knowledge at that time that people were subject only to natural law and the private lives of free men could not be subject to written laws or involuntary servitude. Only commerce and trade was to be affected by government, as commerce and trade would benefit from the protection that government could give. At the time the Constitution and the Bill of Rights were drafted, it was a matter of fact that no written law could be passed that would operate upon the private rights, lives, and property of the individual. All written laws were for the express purpose of the operation of government and related consenting commerce, for the general welfare of the people and country.

The only law that operated upon the private lives of the people was the common law of the land and natural law. The common law of the land is based upon natural law and is discerned by logic and reason. The common law is very simple and takes no great legal mind to comprehend it. The common law is simply the law of damage. If an individual were accused by sworn testimony of inflicting some form of damage, then it is the obligation of the accused to appear in court and plead his case. There were no lengthy written laws that were only decipherable by lawyers or the well-read. The common law is fair to all, in all cases. If there is no damage, there is no crime or reason for lawsuit.

The new government and society were on their way to greatness. The original founding principles of the American form of government created a society that was second-to-none. The freedom of the people caused unprecedented advances in technology, industry, manufacturing, and inventions because the people of America had the freedom and liberty to do whatever they desired, without hindrance from a sovereign master.

> *"The preservation of the sacred fire of liberty, and the destiny of the republican model of government, are justly considered as deeply, perhaps as finally staked, on the experiment entrusted to the hands of the American people."*
> **George Washington**

The Evolution of Common
Law and Written Law

It came to pass that America excelled beyond anyone's wildest dreams. The people of America were free to live as they pleased. Free to exercise their liberties as they saw fit. It was common knowledge among men that all men were subject to the common law. No written laws ruled over the private people. They were able own their own land and homes without payment of rent or taxes to a king. The people governed themselves by the common law based upon natural law. There had to be an infringement upon another's liberties or a damage before any court action could be summoned. The people were judged by juries of their peers by the facts and maxims of law of the case. They simply submitted the facts of the case to be judged by common sense, reason, and the maxims of law.

The written laws (also known as positive law) were essentially types of contracts in which men of commerce and government agreed to do business. These contracts were written down and were called legislative laws, laws of commerce, and laws of government.

Of course, you would have to have written laws, rules, regulations, and the like, to organize and operate government and the military. The government is a form of commerce. It would be impossible to organize government without a structured, written system of rules and regulations. When you organize government into systems, government works more efficient and productive. Although government is run by people, the government itself in not a living, breathing being that was endowed with God-given rights and liberties. Therefore you don't violate any rights of the government by requiring government to abide by the written law.

Commerce is much the same as government. You can compare a company or an organization to a government. They both work more efficiently and productively when they follow written rules and regulations. They both have people that freely volunteer to work and receive benefit from them. When a company or organization becomes more efficient and more productive, it makes more profit and becomes more productive. Profit and productivity are the bottom line for most companies and organizations.

Here is America with thriving businesses and government, all conforming to the system of the written commercial and legislative law. All of these written laws were created while taking into account the common law of damage and common sense. Written laws were created to be as fair as possible with the foundation of these laws being the common law. These written laws were as fair as any contract can be. Of course, as in any contract, the party that failed to live up to the terms of the contract received collateral damage of some sort. The party that failed to perform most often came out on the short end of the stick. Agreeing to something and not performing according to the agreement results in default. This is a basis of common law.

> **"Honesty is the first chapter in the book of Wisdom."**
> **Thomas Jefferson**

Let's compare violating a written law to violating the common law or natural law. A private individual knows by instinct that he is violating the common law. He knows that stealing, murder, destruction of property, etc., violates the common law and natural law. He does not have to read this or have it written down to know it is wrong.

On the other hand, a government worker or company worker must be familiar with the written rules and codes relating to his job to determine if he is breaking a rule. He must learn the process before he can determine whether the process is breaking down because of a degradation of the regimented rules.

Contrary to the private life of an individual, a new worker on a new job who knew nothing of how his organization worked could conceivably break many written rules or laws without his knowledge. On the other hand, it would be difficult for someone to violate natural law or the common law without his knowledge of doing so.

The private man would know nothing of the laws, rules, and regulations of a government entity or company if he was not made familiar with them. On the contrary, a government or company worker can never claim ignorance of the common law or natural law.

> *"Facts are stubborn things; and whatever may be our wishes, our inclinations, or the dictates of our passion, they cannot alter the state of facts and evidence."*
> **John Adams**

Should the private man be required to know all the laws, rules, and regulations of the government or commercial entities if he does not have some kind of contractual relationship with these entities? Of course not!

Should a government or company worker be expected to understand the common law or natural law? Of course he should!

Could written statutory law ever take precedent over common law or natural law? Of course not!

The common law and natural law are determined by logical reason, common sense, and conscience. All written law grows out of common law. The common law is the mother of all written law.

In simple-to-understand terms, the common law is as follows:

You are bound to abide by your contracts and agreements. You can do as you please as long as you do not create damage or an obvious danger to others or to things. You guide your conscience by your common sense and morality.

Now, can you possibly think of any situation where you should be punished for a crime if you abided by, and did not violate, the above description of common law? I think not. This author has tried. If you abide by the common law, you are good member of society.

Why should an employee of the government or a company be expected to be proficient at knowing all the written laws relating to his job? Because he accepted the responsibility of the job and he gets paid to do it. By voluntary consent he has waived many of his natural liberties to be subject to the written law, as he receives a benefit for doing so. That is the nature of any job. When you accept the responsibility of a job, you essentially accept a new master for a period of time during the day and for the benefit of payment. But the driving point is that you decide, accept, and consent. It is your choice and no one by any right or authority can force you to accept or consent.

Would it be right to expect the private man to be subject to the written laws of an entity he has nothing to do with? Of course not.

Would it be right for the umpire of a baseball game to tell the people watching the game what to do out in the parking lot? Of course not.

As we can see, the worker has given up some of his freedoms for his job. He is told when to work and when to leave work, when to have lunch, and the type of clothes to wear. There are negative consequences for failing to obey the written rules (or laws). They come with the territory.

What happens when the worker quits his job? His ex-boss comes to his house and says, "Hey, get up and get your uniform on!" The ex-worker can then get some long, sought satisfaction because all of a sudden all those written laws mean nothing to him. Those written laws have no authority over the ex-worker anymore. Just one day before, the written laws had usurped his rights by voluntary consent, and the next they mean nothing because he has withdrawn his consent.

It is much the same with an individual in the military. When this individual signs up to be in the military, he contractually waives many of his god-given natural rights. He must strictly adhere to the rules and regulations of the military. He must engage in activities that could cost him his life. That is what he agreed to when he joined. This is his contract and agreement with the military.

The military must hold all of its personnel to the written rule for the success and efficiency of its organization. When a soldier has done his time and fulfilled all of his contractual obligations with the military, he is, of course, no longer obligated to the rules and regulations of his former military organization except for what he might have agreed to.

> **"There is no injury which is done with (the injured one's) consent."**
> **Ulpianus**

The evolution of the written laws is not hard to understand. Government and commerce must be structured to be productive. Forming large groups of people into systems of effective productivity is something that requires organization and the written rule. All of the people that belong to such organizations have voluntarily agreed to be a part of those organizations and abide by all of their written rules.

The private man does not need written rules to function freely in the world. No one can write something on a piece of paper and expect the free private man to be subject to it. Just as you could not lawfully force an honest man to go to work against his will, you cannot force the honest man to abide by something that another individual has written on a piece of paper. To do so, would be to force the private man into the obligation of a contract against his will, or, in other words into involuntary servitude. The free private man would have to agree to the contract by voluntary consent or he would be subject to involuntary servitude or a varying degree of slavery or serfdom.

We have established the general consensus that one must, in some way, voluntarily consent to receive a benefit, or to be subject to a written law, rule, regulation, etc... Laws, rules, codes, regulations, and statutes are all forms of contracts to which people often would volunteer to abide by, whether they are read or not.

> **"No man is good enough to govern another man without that other's consent." Abraham Lincoln**

How did it come to pass that so many people in America believe they are subject to written legislative laws? How did it come to pass that so many people are prosecuted and punished for failing to consent? How did it come to pass that even people that work in government (even some ignorant judges), believe that all people are subject to the will of the legislature? How did it come to pass that so many people blindly pay all taxes without question, and in the same breath say they live in a free country? The reasons are many but the solution is simple. Read on, my fellow countrymen, and you will understand why this has happened.

How Written Laws Have Enslaved the People

As we have learned from earlier chapters, written laws (or positive law) are nothing more than governmental contracts by which we can choose to abide or not. We can abide by these laws either by our explicit or presumed consent, or by force and intimidation. Let's examine the different ways with which can we deal with written laws:

We now understand that all written laws only pertain to entities of government and related consenting commerce, and that we can freely choose not to abide by such written laws, thereby reserving all of our natural God-given rights and liberties. In other words, we can explicitly challenge all such presumptions of law and presumed jurisdictions. This is our God-given right as a human being and free American. Remember, we have no master unless we choose one. We can choose to have a master by merely failing to exercise our freedoms and liberties. We can choose to have a master by merely becoming complacent when our liberties are attacked. We can choose to have a master by giving our tacit consent to the presumption of positive law which is claiming title to our God-given rights and liberties. A legal trick has been finely crafted over the years to take advantage of one's lack of due diligence and ignorance of law. This legal trick actually uses principles of common law to trick the people. Read the maxims of law furnished in this book.

Patriotic resistance to this trick is usually met with force and intimidation by enforcers of legislative positive law for two reasons.

One is that the people that work for the enforcement agencies of government are ignorant of the facts and actually do not understand the law well enough to know that legislative positive law does not pertain to the private individual. The ignorance of this enforcement mind-set has evolved through the years because government workers have rarely, if ever, dealt with people who understand law. In court the judge denies the individual due process and a lawful remedy from the oppression thereby giving the slave a good whipping to teach him a lesson he will not soon forget.

The other reason is that the enforcers fully understand that positive law does not pertain to the private individual and will hide the fact that they know. This is what most judges do. They know full well that if it could be proven that they know the truth, they would be found guilty of willful oppression, fraud, and a host of other criminal charges. And there goes that nice government pension with all the perks.

> *"Knowledge is power."*
> **Francis Bacon**

We can deal with positive law by giving our express consent to abide by the written law, voluntarily waive some rights and liberties, and engage in voluntary servitude to our new master. Many people in America believe, for a variety of poorly considered or misguided reasons, that it would be best for them to capitulate to the authority of the written law. Many are actively engaged in public commerce or government and have failed to understand where the line between private and public rights actually begins. It becomes a confusing mess in which they have no place to learn the facts of what is really going on.

> *"It may be true that we can act as we choose, but can we choose?"*
> **J. A. Froude**

Because there is no written curriculum in which to understand the workings of positive and common law, one must reinvent the wheel in order to gain a full understanding of the subject. That is why this book is written in a very easy-to-understand format. If you read this book in its entirety, you will have no problem understanding common law in the future. Common law is easy to understand because it is the law of the people, determined by common sense and logical reasoning.

We can deal with positive law by our presumed or tacit consent. If we fail to rebut or protest the authority of a certain written law, we are presumed by tacit admission to be under the authority of that law. If we fail to protest the authority of a written law, then naturally an enforcement agency will presume that the law pertains to us. Note that no judge has a legal duty to inform a litigant that he has the right to rebut or protest a presumption of law. The judge will not want to upset the delicate balance of the well-oiled legal machine. But the cold hard fact is that all presumptions of law are rebuttable in all courts of law. This is the law. Look up presumption of law in Black's Law Dictionary Sixth Edition and educate yourself.

Positive written law can be forced against our will with the threat of loss of property or threat of imprisonment. This is tyranny at its finest. In America this is usually done in a stealthy manner in which the tyranny is hard to recognize. It is, of course, done in the name of written, legislative, positive law, or statute, which most people have been deceived into believing, is true law. The rebellious individual will feel all alone when confronting this intimidation. This condition causes the rebellious individual to question whether or not what he is doing is right or worth the effort.

Individuals can most often be compelled to comply with the authority of the written law because they do not understand the principles of natural law or the common law. They are further afraid of the intimidation or punishment that comes in response to this resistance. After they have been thoroughly whipped by judges denying them due process, punishment, and fines, most people feel the monster is too big to tackle and feel that someone else should take it on. Most people can only take a beating for so long before giving up. It takes a real American to dig in, organize, prepare, and fight for freedom and liberty.

The most important thing to understand is that all lawmaking bodies in America, whether they be federal, state or local, only have authority to make laws, rules and regulations that pertain to government and related consenting commerce, such as corporations, licensed entities, the military, etc. They absolutely have no authority to make laws that pertain to the private lives of honest, common law-abiding people. They are not our masters or dictators! To put it another way, there is absolutely no documentation authorizing any government agency to exercise authority over private sovereign individuals against their will and without their consent.

This presumed authority has crept into our lives so slowly over time that we never realized it ever began.

> *"I believe there are more instances of the abridgment of the freedom of the people by gradual and silent encroachments of those in power than by violent and sudden usurpations."*
> **James Madison**

The sole reason for our founding fathers to create our American form of government was for the promotion of trade, the protection of our borders, and the protection of the natural rights and property of the people of the country. There was never any intent or authorization by God or our founding fathers to rule the private lives and property of the free honest people of America. Ruling the private lives of the people was for kings and dictators. This was exactly what America was created to guard against. The private lives of all common law abiding people of America are to have unrestricted liberty, subject only to natural law.

In fact, it must be expressly noted that our founding fathers fought a war with England to get away from the same oppression and tyranny that seems to be an accepted everyday occurrence today. The principles of true freedom and liberty were so ingrained in the people of those days that it would have been redundant and tautological to mention it in our founding documents. It would have been like mentioning in a medical journal that people need to breathe air to stay alive. It was common knowledge to all people in those days.

Our founding fathers never dreamed that the people of today would accept such feudalism without concern. The forced obligations that the people of today accept would have astonished the people of that era. It was just a matter of common sense and logical thinking of the time, which no one was subject to the authority of another without their consent.

> *"No man is good enough to govern another man without that other's consent."*
>
> **Abraham Lincoln**

Our original Bill of Rights was merely a general instruction, reminder, and contractual agreement to the newly-formed American government concerning how to respect the God-given rights and liberties of the people of America. Remember that the people receive their rights from God, not the Constitution. In other words the people were born with inherent rights. Rights that cannot be taken away unless imprisoned for a crime.

When an entity accepts the responsibility of becoming a government entity or accepts the benefits of becoming a corporation or licensed entity, it agrees to abide by the written laws, rules, and regulations that have been established to govern and regulate such entities. Essentially, the entity has contractually agreed to subject itself to the authority of the positive laws governing its commercial activity.

Entities of government or related consenting commerce are one case, but what about the private lives of the individual?

The first fact that must be realized is that all written laws created by American government can only have legitimate authority over the private individual with the consent of that individual. This can be by expressed consent or by presumed consent, which is most often the case since the private individual is ignorant of the design of the presumptions of law. In other words, the average individual is clueless about the procedures of rebutting the presumptions of law upon which most authorities rely on to enforce the positive law upon the private individual. Secondly, even those private individuals who are knowledgeable enough to understand this legal trickery are most often not willing to take the chance or spend the valuable time and resources to learn about and assert their rights. This is the linchpin to the whole fraud that is usurping the rights of the people.

> *"I have always thought the actions of men the best interpreters of their thoughts."*
>
> **John Locke**

It must become second nature to recognize when an individual is forced against his will to abide by a written law or forced obligations. The mere act of enforcement is nothing but tyranny and oppression against that individual.

Thinking in the light of natural law and reason, how can another individual (such as a member of a legislative body) write something on a piece of paper, call it a law or regulation, and force others to abide by such a law without the consent of the individual? These government employees have no authority over anyone's rights, liberties or property.

Where did the lawmaker obtain such awesome authority to be able to force others to abide by the will of the lawmaking body? Upon what document is the lawmaker relying for such authority? The fact of the matter is that the lawmaker has no such authority over private people and relies solely on the voluntary or presumed consent of the people. The lawmaking body also relies on the consent of commercial entities. No one forces a company to incorporate. No one forces a person to become licensed. They do it voluntarily.

Anyone of rational thought and reason can conclude that, if an individual is forced to give his time, money, property, services, or performance against his will, then the individual has lost his true freedom and liberty. He is subject to involuntary servitude and is nothing more than a slave.

Let's look at the simple case of the income tax. The IRS intimidates the private individual into subjecting his labor to the IRS (money is labor.) The natural law of an individual's right to his labor is violated by forcing the individual to give part of his labor to the IRS. Essentially, the individual is forced to work for the benefit of the IRS for free, against his will. If the individual refuses to capitulate to the demands of the IRS, further violation of his natural rights will be imposed in the form of penalties and/or incarceration.

> *"The hardest thing to understand in the world is the income tax."*
>
> **Albert Einstein**

If the purpose of government is only to regulate itself and related consenting commerce for the protection of the natural rights and property of the people, how can it be that the government can violate the natural rights of people? The answer is that it makes no sense at all. The government has evolved into such a mixed-up and convoluted mess that it has missed the intent of its original creation. It is actually an insult to the intelligence of any rational thinking individual.

The reason why average Americans have never realized this before is because they never had a chance to put it in proper perspective in order to analyze the situation properly. The American people have never had an organized curriculum for understanding common law until now. As was stated in the introduction of this book, you will begin to put all the familiar pieces of the puzzle together in order to see the entire picture. If you have read all of this book to this point, what does the picture look like to you now?

Of course, there are those who will make the futile argument that if we do not give up some of our freedoms and subject ourselves to written law, society will fall into a state of anarchy or lawlessness. This ludicrous idea is most often intended to compel recipients to be instilled with fear and insecurity in order to cause them to submit their private lives to the trickery of government authority.

The truth of the matter is that you cannot have anarchy and lawlessness unless you violate the common law. When people abide by the rules of natural and common law, anarchy and lawlessness is impossible. One must understand that futile argument is not logical and is merely the product of a poorly considered personal opinion.

> *"All propaganda has to be popular and has to adapt its spiritual level to the perception of the least intelligent of those towards whom it intends to direct itself."*
> *"The great masses of the people . . . will more easily fall victims to a big lie than to a small one."*
> **Adolf Hitler**

Rational thinking concludes that there can only be anarchy and lawlessness when people infringe upon the rights of others, against the dictates of natural law and the common law of the land. Anarchy does not happen because people violate written or positive law. Anarchy only happens when people violate natural law. In fact, it is often the case that the enforcement of written positive law violates natural law and the rights of the private individual. Such was the case with the true life story of Dave and Lisa discussed in the earlier chapter.

The other propaganda argument is that "we will not have any money for roads and schools if we don't give up some of our liberties." This uniformed and ignorant fabrication is ludicrous at best.

First and foremost, the government was only given taxing authority over consenting commercial entities in the form of tariffs, sales tax, gas tax, etc. The government has no authority to tax the private individual without his or her consent.

For example, a store raises the price of its items in relation to the tax that the store consents to send to the government. The consenting commercial entity pays the tax to the government and passes the price increase on to the consumer. The consumer only pays an increase in the price of the product because of the tax. It is an illusion that the consumer pays the sales tax. The consenting commercial entity collects and pays the tax.

Let's examine the case of property tax. The government may pass legislation that requires a commercial lending institution to pay a property tax because the lending institution holds equitable title to the property it lent money on. The lending institution passes the cost on to the borrower during the term of the loan through an impound account. Once the loan is paid off, there is no authority that can force the private homeowner to continue to pay the property tax. It is an unfathomable rights violation to force an individual to pay the government to live and exist in his own home or lose his home for non-compliance. Yet it happens because it is one of the main cash cows for the government.

Just because the government has been forcefully extorting money from private people for years in the form of property and income taxes does not make it lawful, moral, just, or right, any more than a mobster collecting protection money would be right because he had been doing it for years. Rights and liberties of people are not negotiable in American society. The propaganda that our country will go broke without taxes is totally false and literally impossible, as explained in the next chapter on money.

Understanding Our American Money System

American economics must be understood to effectively remedy a big part of America's ills. The money issue alone could be the subject of an entire book. But in a nutshell, we will examine the situation in a brief and easy-to-understand way.

Part of the foundation of understanding America's monetary system is to understand that the Federal Reserve Bank (FED) is a privately owned bank. The FED is not owned by the U.S. government. The Federal Reserve Bank is not federal and it has no reserves. The Federal Reserve Bank was named to give the illusion of being a federally owned institution. Most people erroneously believe that the FED is owned by the government and is a government institution. This belief is false and a big con game on the people of America.

According to the dictates of the Constitution, our government has no authority to allow the U.S. Treasury to print money (bank notes) for the privately owned Federal Reserve Bank. Our government has no authority to allow a private bank to control America's money. The government receives no beneficial interest for the FED to control and own America's money. The FED is a privately owned bank that received its status as a national bank in 1913 through fraud and payoffs.

Our founding fathers knew very well that a country should never allow a private bank to gain control of a country's money or the bank would eventually control the country. That is why the Constitution dictates that only Congress shall mint and coin money.

> **"That man is admired above all men, who is not influenced by money."**
>
> **Cicero De Officiis**

In 1913 the Federal Reserve Act was passed into law, giving complete control of America's money supply to the privately owned Federal Reserve Bank. The crooked politicians that voted in the Federal Reserve Act of 1913 figured they could squeak by the Constitution because the money would still be printed by the U.S. Treasury. They effectively bypassed the original intent of the Constitution, which states that the government should own its own money, not print bank notes for a private bank.

Now our government prints Federal Reserve Notes instead of United States Notes as it did up until 1913. The Federal Reserve Bank pays the U.S. Treasury three cents on the dollar to pay for the printing costs of the Federal Reserve (bank) Notes. The FED does not put up any collateral for the principle of the notes. It does not have to put any gold into Fort Knox for the principle of the money printed. The FED acquires the money for free minus printing costs, while reaping the benefits of having the principle and interest paid back by borrowers. Remember, the FED does not pay for the principle of the money in the first place. They merely have it printed and lend it into circulation.

The FED's financial books have never been audited and there is no requirement to do so. The FED lends the money back to the U.S. Government and this debt is known as the National Debt. The Fed also lends money to the people, businesses and other countries through their member lending institutions and banks. The government and other borrowers then pay back the principle and interest to the private FED. The FED receives all the benefit of the money while our government merely goes deeper into a debt that should not exist in the first place. This deal should be criminal. It is the biggest fraud ever perpetrated in the civilized world.

If the above-mentioned was not bad enough, every dime of income tax collected from the people goes to pay the FED for the fictionally created National Debt while the government borrows its operating money from the FED, causing the National Debt to become that much larger.

The question is what would cause our country to become stronger: using bank notes or United States Notes?

Think of it this way: If you had a ranch, would you be better off with plenty of money for projects and to lend to your ranch hands, or would you be better off owing money to the bank for the ranch and everything in it, plus having to borrow money from the bank for anything purchased by the ranch? Does anyone need to contemplate this question?

If our government were printing United States Notes as lawfully required by the dictates of the Constitution instead of printing private Federal Reserve (bank) Notes, then the money would be owned by the U.S. government instead of the privately owned FED. The government would then lend the money to the FED, which would lend the money to the people, as it was originally intended by our founding documents.

The government would receive the benefit of all the principle and interest of the money that is lent into circulation, instead of the FED bank. All of the money would eventually go back to the government as the loans were paid back.

The government would not have a national debt and would have more money than it would ever need to operate and lend back to the people. This would certainly be more money than could be collected in unlawful taxes. This means no taxes, no forced obligations, and plenty of money for projects that promote humanity and create jobs.

For a very informed study of our money supply and banking systems, it is suggested that one watch the documentary "Money Masters" and "Monopoly Men". These documentaries can easily be found by searching on the Web by their names.

There would be no valid reasoning to stealthily extort unlawful taxes from private people, because all of the principle of the money lent to the people would go to the government instead of to the privately owned Federal Reserve Bank. The entire concept of extorting money from the people would end, thus creating more justice and prosperity in American society.

It is not the fault of the private people that our government has allowed the FED to own America's money against the dictates of our Constitution. It is merely a bad situation that needs rectification for the sake of our country. The people are not obligated to forfeit any of their freedoms or liberties (money) because of this fraudulent scheme.

So don't let ignorant people convince you of their propaganda that you must give up some of your freedoms and liberties or the country will go broke. The idea that the country would go broke is a total fabrication and is literally impossible. Remember, all money is not backed by anything but the "good faith and credit of the Federal Government. Money is merely created out of thin air and lent into circulation. Money is only a tool for exchanging value. There is simply no valid reason for government to usurp the rights and liberties of the people for want of money. Plus, it is unlawful.

> *"The art of taxation consists in so plucking the goose as to obtain the largest amount of feathers with the least possible amount of hissing."*
> **Louis XIV**

Oppression and tyranny is essentially an act of war against the people who it oppresses. The only reason this stealthy oppression and tyranny can thrive in America is that the majority of people are complacent and ignorant of these subjects. The majority of people put up with such oppression and tyranny out of fear, intimidation, or because they actually believe that they must submit to the demands of legislative authority. It all boils down to the fact that the principles of natural law have been long forgotten by most of the people. Most of the people in America actually believe that they are subject to written positive law and that they have to pay taxes or the country will go broke. If people really understood what is happening, there would be a lot more Americans fighting to repair our flawed government.

As we can plainly see, an individual forced to obey a written law absent his consent has been effectively enslaved by the usurping authority. No excuses for want of money, protection, or any other reason, can justify any act that usurps the rights of honest, free people without their consent.

> *"This country, with its institutions, belongs to the people who inhabit it. Whenever they shall grow weary of the existing government, they can exercise their constitutional right of amending it, or their revolutionary right to dismember or overthrow it."*
>
> **Abraham Lincoln**

Understanding Freedom, Liberty, and Natural Law

It is of the utmost importance that the reader has a full and thorough understanding of freedom, liberty and natural law. These terms are quite often used loosely and without true reflection. It is unlikely that the average high-school or college student could accurately define the important aspects of freedom and liberty. Without a solid understanding of these words, an individual can easily be compelled into different forms of slavery or involuntary servitude.

The proper understanding of freedom and liberty according to natural law is imperative to understanding the lawful authority and rights of government. The natural law of justice is discovered by reason and common sense. In a state of nature, we are forbidden to interfere with the lives of others, except to do justice on an offender of natural law. Natural law, which is deduced by reason and common sense, teaches all sane people that all are equal and forbids injury to another's life, freedom, liberty, health, or possessions.

A state of perfect freedom and liberty according to natural law allows an individual to do with his actions, possession and persons, anything he may see fit, without the consent or approval of any other individual, government, or human power. And, of course, the law of nature dictates that he may not create damage, violate the rights or possessions of others, or create an obvious danger, in the course of exercising his true freedoms and liberties.

> *"You cannot possibly have a broader basis for any government than that which includes all the people, with all their rights in their hands, and with an equal power to maintain their rights."*
> **William Lloyd Garrison**

In other words, if you were stranded on a long-forgotten island with a group of people, any individual in the group could do whatever he so desired as long as he did not create an obvious danger or infringe upon or damage anything or anyone with malicious intent or negligence. Try to imagine how someone in the group could do something worthy of punishment if he did not violate this natural law. The group could prosper and live out their lives, living by natural law, without any conflict, fighting, or war if no one violated natural law.

Before there could be any conflict, someone would have to create damage, create danger, or infringe upon the liberties of others. If everyone always abided by natural law, of course, there would be no need for the group to create any written laws or rules except for those for the organization, promotion, and prosperity of whatever commerce or trade they may establish between themselves. Such rules or laws made between members of the group would be nothing more than private contracts or agreements.

So indeed, if we have established that natural law is God's law and is just law, then we have to conclude that the principles of natural law should always take precedence over positive law. It should always be recognized that all positive laws grow out of a foundation of natural law. Any positive law that violates the principles of natural law would, of course, be an unjust, bad, and invalid law.

It is absurd to justify the enforcement of a man-made positive law if indeed that positive law violates natural law. Yet it happens on a daily basis in today's application of positive law by government agencies.

Would it be right or lawful to take away an individual's freedom and/or possessions when he had not infringed upon, damaged, or proven dangerous to others? Of course it would be wrong. Denying someone their freedoms and possessions is a violation of natural law in itself, except to do justice on an offender of natural law.

> *"America, with the same voice which spoke herself into existence as a nation, proclaimed to mankind the inextinguishable rights of human nature, and the only lawful foundations of government."*
> **John Quincy Adams**

Equality according to the law of nature is a state of uniformity in which all powers and jurisdictions are equally reciprocal among the people. It means no man is subject to subordination or subjection to another unless it is by his voluntary consent. It is a basic maxim of natural law that cannot be taken by force or by any lawful jurisdiction. Might does not make right.

If a band of murdering robbers were to take control of a town and its people, by God's law and the law of nature, the people of that town are not lawfully subject to the will of the robbers. The people of the town might only consent by force, for their survival.

A robber holding a gun to your head and forcing you to sign away deeds to your property would never give lawful title to the robber, nor would it take lawful title away from you. There is a basic maxim of law that any contract that is agreed to under threat, duress, or coercion is a void contract.

I challenge the reader to imagine a situation in which an individual is deemed guilty of a crime when he has not created damage, created an obvious danger, or infringed upon the liberties of anyone. If this were a perfect world and everyone in it lived by the natural law, then there would be no need for written law, except for the organization and regulation of government and commerce.

Of course we do not live in a perfect world so we must put into perspective the interactive relationships between natural law and positive law. For a just and fair society, no one must be allowed to violate natural law, whether it is a petty crook, king, cop, priest, lawmaker, politician, or government.

> **"The world is a dangerous place to live, not because of the people who are evil, but because of the people who don't do anything about it."**
>
> **Albert Einstein**

One must always remember that any positive law that violates natural law is a void law, regardless of the excuses or arguments made for the need of such positive law. The diligent exercise of this simple maxim of natural law will do more for the preservation of honest and just government if the people demand that it is upheld. Imagine if all people of America stood hard and fast against any positive law that violated natural law. America would become stronger and more just than when it was created by our honorable founding fathers. It is now the right time in history for this to happen. Our technology and moral values have evolved to the point where we can unfold this maxim into a reality.

According to common law and the dictates of our Constitution, before anyone can lawfully be accused of and prosecuted for any crime, a sworn affidavit must be produced detailing the damage that was created. The important thing to remember here is that there must be real damage of some kind. This simple lawful process was common knowledge among people in the early days of our country. Most people today, however, are ignorant of these important founding principles of law and quite often waive their right to this due process by tacit consent. Any tacit consent that violates the rights of an individual is the result of fraudulent deception. Even so, it is the duty of the victim to do his own due diligence. This is why it is vitally important for the general population to understand the basis of natural law as readily as it is able to read, write, and do math. Without such general knowledge of the law, rights and liberties will just keep slipping away. Just like in the old saying, "If you do not know what your rights are, you don't have any." There was never a truer statement.

If you take exception to what you have just read, you must reflect on the reasons for your objections and honestly evaluate your opposition and contentions. If you do not, you are in a state of denial that will forever keep you from thinking clearly on this subject.

You have the right to do so if you so desire, so long as your state of denial does not infringe upon or harm others. In other words, you have the right to believe any way you please, but you have no right to force your beliefs on others.

> *"Insanity: Doing the same thing over and over again and expecting different results."*
>
> **Albert Einstein**

The Relationship Between Positive Law and Natural Law

As previously discussed, positive law is enacted by lawmaking bodies for the operation of government and relating consenting commerce. One must remember that all lawmaking bodies in America only have authority to make laws, rules, and regulations that pertain to government and related commerce. There is no authority or power granted to lawmaking bodies to have power over any honest private individual unless by consent of that individual. If they had such authority, they would hold the power of a dictator or king and would violate maxims of law. This is not only the law, but a maxim of logical thought and reasoning.

Positive laws are all written laws that are enacted and written by lawmaking bodies, as distinguished from the unwritten common law of the land, which is based upon natural law and maxims of law. Common law is the form and procedure in which natural law is presented in the courts. Common law is based on natural law, and is the common right of all people. All people have a right to rely on common law to defend their natural rights. The common law cannot lawfully be denied to the people by the courts, even though it is happening all the time.

In theory, all positive law is supposed to be based on a foundation of common law. This means that no positive law can violate a maxim of law or the rights of the free people. I say "free people" in order to exclude convicted criminals. When a criminal has been duly convicted of a crime, the government has lawfully acquired jurisdiction over the criminal and therefore can use positive law to dictate his punishment and usurp his rights lawfully.

It has come to pass that through the ignorance of the people regarding law; the practice of common law in the courts has almost completely been forgotten and is rarely used. Therefore, positive law has evolved to a point in which many times positive law usurps the principles of natural law. The principles of natural law are the maxims of law, many of which are listed at the end of this text.

Due to the fact that positive law has become so complicated and convoluted, most people must hire an attorney to handle their affairs in court. Attorneys are mandated by the courts to use the rules of civil and criminal procedure in their practice of law. These procedures are for the express purpose of governing the professional conduct of attorneys and must be learned through extensive study. These procedures forbid the use of common law procedure in licensed attorneys' practices. Remember, private people that are not licensed to practice law, have the right to demand common law jurisdiction in courts of law. This is the supreme right of the people guaranteed by the Bill of Rights, regardless of the arbitrary opinions of any judge that may say otherwise.

Therefore, since most cases are handled by licensed attorneys, common law procedure in the courts has become a long-forgotten dinosaur. Just as you would forget anything that you had not used in many years, many judges themselves have forgotten common law procedure since they never see it in their court rooms. Consequently, positive law has evolved into a mere perversion of the original intent in which it was created.

In fact, most courts have become so ignorant of the common law, that they will resist common law actions. The courts will quite often continue to treat a case brought forth in common law jurisdiction as a statutory case and which must abide by the rules of positive law and procedure rather than by the dictates of established maxims of law.

Most people believe that the courts would not steer them wrong, so they are swayed into tacitly consenting into the jurisdiction of positive law instead of claiming their natural right to common law jurisdiction. These people do not realize that they have been legally tricked into waiving their natural right to rely on maxims of law and due process to protect their rights.

It is also a common trick among attorneys and courts to attempt to trick a common-law plaintiff or defendant into statutory jurisdiction by continuing to treat a common law action as a statutory action, in the hope that the common law litigant will comply by ignorance, confusion, intimidation, or that he will just simply give up.

> *"It is a maxim among lawyers that whatever hath been done before may legally be done again: and therefore they take special care to record all the decisions formerly made against common justice and the general reason of mankind. These, under the name of precedents, they produce as authorities to justify the most iniquitous opinions; and the judges never fail of directing accordingly."*
>
> **Jonathan Swift**

It is important to remember that the District Courts and Supreme Court have two distinct jurisdictions: common-law jurisdiction and statutory jurisdiction. These courts cannot hear a case in both jurisdictions. That is why it is so important to always continue to assert common-law jurisdiction whenever you are involved in an action in the courts. If you fail to assert common law jurisdiction, you leave yourself wide open to having your rights usurped by legislative law.

Always make it perfectly clear that you do not grant any authority to any statutory or legislative jurisdictions. A common law litigant must always remain strictly in the common-law jurisdiction of the court in order to hold such jurisdiction. Remember that a court hearing can be remanded into common law jurisdiction if any party to the action is a private individual that demands so. All private individuals are entitled to have matters of inherent rights heard in common-law jurisdiction, even though today's court system will do everything in its power to convince you otherwise.

Common law jurisdiction is straightforward and deduced by common sense and reason, and is based on the facts and maxims of law presented in a case. Whereas positive law is comprised thousands of different written laws, rules, and regulations which were enacted by lawmakers that know nothing about the particular case in which the rules are being used. In fact, attorneys very rarely concern themselves with the facts of the case, and rely heavily on the presentation of rules and regulations of positive law or the violations of those rules.

In a court of statutory jurisdiction, natural law and maxims of law are often violated because of the presumption that the parties are subject to positive law. The rights, property, and justice for the people are secondary to the rules and regulations enacted by a lawmaking body. True justice is seldom achieved in statutory jurisdiction.

> *"Reason is the life of the law; nay, the common law itself is nothing else but reason. . . The law, which is perfection of reason."*
>
> **Sir Edward Coke**

As we have learned, no one has the lawful right to violate natural law. The right of a government to punish must only be derived from the right to punish found in natural law. For a government to have the right to punish any other way would be a right derived against the law of nature and God.

For first-time discoverers of sovereignty, the fine details of how to litigate in common law would be way over their heads, even though it is basically very simply. Just like reading would be impossible without learning the alphabet. How to actually fight and defend cases in courts of law is the subject of another book. The point of this book is to cause the reader to understand the foundational principles of personal sovereignty and the basic core principles of law that America was founded on. It is important to realize that even if you never bring a case to court, it is your duty as an American to understand the principles propounded in this book.

> *"Freedom is the right to choose: the right to create for oneself the alternatives of choice. Without the possibility of choice and the exercise of choice a man is not a man but a member, an instrument, a thing."*
>
> **Archibald Macleish**

Once You Understand the Problem, What Do You Do?

If you have read this entire book up to this point and fully understand its contents, you probably understand what is needed for ridding our American government of the cancer that is destroying the lives of our fellow Americans and the integrity of this great nation.

The use of common law is a very simple process. It does not take great intelligence. It does not require volumes of reading and studying. It does not take a law degree or attorney. What it takes is the use of your common sense, the ability to effectively present evidence and facts, and the desire to stop unjust oppression. What is takes is the guts to stand up and say "Prove you have the right to force this claim on me".

When the word *God* is mentioned in this book, it does not necessarily mean any one particular god of any one religion. *God* can simply mean the natural order of things or the creative energy of our universe. Whatever *God* means to you is how you should interpret the word in this text. The point is to not get into any type of religious debate relating to the meaning of the word *God* as used in this text.

> *"I believe in one God and no more, and I hope for happiness beyond this life. I believe in the equality of man; and I believe that religious duties consist in doing justice, loving mercy, and endeavoring to make our fellow creatures happy."*
>
> **Thomas Paine**

Always remember this all-important maxim: Once you fully understand the problems and questions, the answers and solutions will be bestowed upon you in the simplest possible form. In other words, if you are informed enough to thoroughly understand the problem, then you are informed enough to realize the answers to the problem. If you cannot realize the answers to the problems, than you do not thoroughly understand the problem. This may not make sense to you now, but give it time and you will realize the truth in these words.

Just as in nature everything takes the path of least resistance, so will the answers come in the simplest possible form. Sometimes the answers will be so simple that they will slip right past you without your notice of them. Sometimes the answers will be so simple that you will refuse to believe them to be true. It is usually the human element that causes the answers to appear more difficult than they really are.

Remember this one all inspiring fact: The information in this book will cause you to discover your free, sovereign mentality and cause your remedy to come in the simplest of ways. Nothing about the subject of sovereignty and common law will appear complicated when you fully understand the concepts brought forth in this book. To be a true sovereign American who is instrumental in protecting the foundational principles of freedom and liberty of this country, one must understand sovereignty and stay persistently vigilant to protect it.

> *"Nothing in this world can take the place of persistence. Talent will not; nothing is more common than unsuccessful people with talent. Genius will not; unrewarded genius is almost a proverb. Education will not; the world is full of educated derelicts. Persistence and determination alone are omnipotent. The slogan 'press on' has solved and always will solve the problems of the human race."*
> **Calvin Coolidge**

Let's begin with a general example concerning an enforcement authority that is unjustly attempting to assert a claim against someone against his will. The following scenario is a typical case. Remember, this is a general text-book example for educational purposes to drive home the principles propounded in this text. This is to illustrate how a lawful process should proceed in a perfect world.

Let's assume a government enforcement officer (e.g., cop, code enforcement, IRS, or animal control) approaches a sovereign individual verbally or by writing, and demands that he provide some form of involuntary servitude (e.g., money, time or services) for the benefit of his agency. He tells the sovereign individual that he must comply because it is the law. One must keep in mind that the officer probably knows nothing of common law and believes that all people are subject to positive law merely because he himself is subject to positive law during his employment.

What is the remedy or defense?

1. The very first thing you must do is ask the officer if there is a valid sworn complaint describing damage for which you are being accused of. If there is a sworn complaint or evidence of damage, it would be wise to exercise good will by offering assistance and helping to rectify the damage. At all times reserve your rights, but show good faith. If there is no damage or valid charging instrument or complaint, the officer is attempting to persuade you to volunteer into legislative jurisdiction. You might tell the officer that, since there is no damage or valid complaint, he has no authority to bother you and bid him good day. If the officer attempts to force legislative law upon you, step 2 would be a logical sequence of events worthy of achieving justice for the betterment of society and government.
2. Common sense, logic, and rational thinking will cause you to ask the enforcement officer who he is and on what contractual agreement he is relying to determine that you owe his agency anything. Further, on what documentation is the officer relying to determine that you are subject to the law he is attempting to enforce. It is prudent to inform the officer that he is in error when he presumes that you are subject to the legislative law he is attempting to enforce upon you. It is equally important to

tell the officer that you are not consenting, and that you do not intend to consent to any of the officer's forced obligations.

> **"I never give them hell. I just tell the truth, and they think it is hell."**
> **Harry S. Truman**

3. Ask to see a valid contract or agreement with your signature attached, or a valid warrant based on a sworn statement alleging that you have created some form of damage and stating what that damage actually is. Ask the officer what his "probable cause" is to investigate you. It must be ingrained in you that for any lawful process to be valid there must be some form of valid contract or valid complaint based upon a sworn statement of facts that you have created some form of damage or are subject to some agreement. If there is no such valid contract or warrant, there is no lawful authority acting upon you.

4. You may also ask the enforcement officer for documentation of proof of the officer's authority to even deal with you on the subject he has brought up. You must always challenge all presumed authority in order to protect your rights and liberties. If you fail to challenge a presumed authority, you give your tacit consent to such authority. It is a basic maxim of law that any authority that is lawfully challenged holds the burden of proving such authority. It is also a maxim of law that if one does not challenge the presumed authority that one is tacitly admitting by silence to be subject to the presumed authority.

5. You also have the right to demand documentation of proof that the lawmaking body has authority over your private life or possessions absent your consent. One will always find that the simple questions and requests will never be answered because there are simply no lawful answers that can be given. They have no lawful claim. There is no one in government that has jurisdiction over your inherent rights, period!

It is the duty of all government officials to answer the questions brought forth above. It is also the duty of all government officials to prove jurisdiction when challenged.

A government entity cannot lawfully violate maxims of law, rights, and liberties, except by the consent of the victim. If government does usurp rights, evidence should be gathered and the violation should be exposed in a court of competent jurisdiction and other managing agencies.

When, thousands of people begin protecting their rights and improving government in this manner, the truth will come out and justice will prevail. We will have a more effective government for our efforts. This is the only proper and effective way to correct poor government. It is up to the people to defend their personal liberties and correct their government until it becomes commonplace and second nature to that society. Remember, all individuals have to protect their own rights and liberties. There will never be legislation to do it for them.

Remember, it is not us against them. The government is not our enemy. The government is a necessity to large societies. It is our government that we need to correct. It is our right and duty to do so. If we witness the government usurping rights and fail to do anything about it, we have allowed it to happen and it is partly our fault.

> *"You need only reflect that one of the best ways to get yourself a reputation as a dangerous citizen these days is to go about repeating the very phrases which our founding fathers used in the struggle for independence."*
> **Charles Austin Beard**

These are the basic simple steps to take in most cases, whether they are said verbally or requested in writing. Yes, it is that simple. As it seems to be in nature, "All of the answers to the greatest questions will appear in the simplest possible form." Everything in the five steps above is nothing but pure un-refutable common sense. Never waiver, and have courage. Stick to your guns and demand proof of any and all claims and presumed authorities that attempt to usurp any of your rights. It is your duty to America, your posterity, and humanity to protect your freedoms and liberties. If you cave in because you are afraid of the consequences, you are not doing what is expected of a true American.

Remember that our forefathers risked their families, lives, lands, businesses, and possessions to free this country from English oppression, and that it was not even close to the amount of oppression the people endure in America today. They would not look kindly on people who did not protect this valuable inheritance.

Don't be naive and expect tyrants and ignorant government employees to roll over for you. It will most often be a fight until they realize that you are serious and will not back down. Show them the mistakes they are making. Let them know that you are actively attempting to correct a malfunction in the proper operation of government. Let them know that you are attempting to build a strong and just government. When there is truth on your side it gives you the strength and perseverance to continue until you have achieved your goal.

> *"Without justice, courage is weak."*
> **Benjamin Franklin**

It is always advisable to get some form of verification that a challenge to authority has been made, either by registered mail, receipt of copy, third-party service, tape recordings, or any other method that would serve as proof in a court of law. Evidence of proof is title to a claim in courts of law.

Be prepared to encounter judges who make bad, arbitrary decisions, who are incompetent and ignorant of common law, or who are just plain corrupt. They are out there and the only way to win is to wear them down with truth, facts, and maxims of law. Filing complaints against bad judges is always an effective avenue as it documents poor decision making by the judge. After a while a bad judge will start to show incompetence and corruption in the face of overwhelming evidence that is contrary to his decisions.

These are things that we must do as Americans to save our crumbling, unethical government and society from eventual ruin. If we allow our government to continue on this path, we will have a government like China, which has total control over the people. We have a duty to save this country. It starts by saving our own personal liberties first. Personal liberty is the end result of government.

No, they can't just steal a few liberties because someone says it is best for the country. This is the propaganda that has caused the erosion of our freedoms in the first place.

Use your head and be careful. Don't be foolish with your survival. It is understandable that there may be situations where attempting to protect your rights would negatively effect the quality of life of your family, loved ones or your livelihood. You may be up against very powerful and corrupt people. It may not be worth the consequences to go head on. One of the main strategies of attorneys and the legal world is to collaterally attack an individual, to cut off his way of survival until he capitulates. It is always wise to protect yourself and your own first. Don't be foolish when it comes to your survival. Be a smart freedom fighter, but be a freedom fighter. Freedom fighters will win in the end, just as our founding fathers did. George Washington had lost every battle until he crossed that frozen Delaware river on that cold dark Christmas night. Good will eventually prevail over evil.

But there are other ways to help correct your government if you are in such a position. You can support and contribute what you can to sovereign rights organizations such as the Sovereign Rights Protection Coalition, infowars.com or We the People Foundation. You can support people and organizations that are actively attempting to correct government. It is important that people do something that helps the cause of re-establishing freedom and liberty in America. If you know you are always doing something, it is a good contribution to society.

> *"Freedom is that instant between when someone tells you to do something and when you decide how to respond."*
> **Dr. Jeffrey Borenstein**

There may be times when you might feel like you are the only one fighting for freedom. You may feel like one piranha fish attempting to take down a giant water buffalo. One piranha only makes a small difference. But there is hope that many more patriotic Americans will realize the way to true freedom, liberty, and a just society. And some day it will not be just one piranha that will be taking down the water buffalo. Thousands will swarm on the water buffalo like a cloud of locusts. And the water buffalo will finally fall prey to the Piranha. And when it does, the people of America will find their salvation and justice in sovereignty and common law. And America's example of justice in common law will become an inspiration for the entire world to marvel at and pattern after, just as it once was before attorneys, banks and positive law stealthily took advantage of the trust of the American people and their ignorance of common law.

Just as the water buffalo cannot survive among thousands of Piranha fish, neither can the stealthy tyrants within our government survive among thousands of decent people hell-bent on protecting their freedoms and correcting their government. Every dedicated American that asserts his God-given rights is just another leak in the dyke of statutory oppression. And the little boy only has so many fingers to stick in those leaks.

"Little strokes fell great oaks."
Benjamin Franklin

It may be that some of the so-called tyrants are as ignorant of the situation as all of the rest of the population. It is possible that, when this common sense is revealed to all and is taught in our schools, the so-called tyrants will do the right thing and respect the rights and liberties of the people. I'm sure they have grandchildren too. It might be that only a small percentage of the tyrants are really tyrants and the rest are just ignorant of what they are really doing.

Look at it this way. Fighting for your freedoms through courts of law is a hell of a lot easier and more effective than rushing a machine-gun nest on the beaches of Normandy or a tunnel rat in Viet Nam. And let it be known to all: Our only salvation is the ability to exercise our freedoms in courts of law. The people will have no chance against the modern weaponry of the government. Armed insurrection is pointless, counter-productive, and suicidal. And after the dust has cleared the same tyrants will do the same thing over again because there is no foundation of law to build a proper government.

One important thing to remember is that no government officer who wishes to keep his job will blatantly tell you publicly that government has authority over your private life and affairs unless of course he is completely ignorant and is doomed to lose his job anyway.

Foundational Principles of Common Law

T here are some basic foundational principles of common law with which you must familiarize yourself in order to understand how to assert the common law in your everyday life, as well as through the courts. You must become proficient at understanding the basic maxims of law in order to defend your rights against statutory oppression. Yes, the common law will actually bring out truth and justice of any case. When you become proficient at understanding the principles of common law you will be able to cause the law to move through the courts according to the truth, justice, and the facts of the case.

> *"Injustice anywhere is a threat to justice everywhere. We are caught in an inescapable network of mutuality, tied in a single garment of destiny. Whatever affects one directly, affects all indirectly."*
>
> **Marin Luther King, Jr.**

First and foremost, one must develop a proper understanding of the maxims of law. Some of the more important and relevant maxims are listed below. It is wise to hang a copy of the maxims of law on your wall. All children should understand these laws. They are as follows:

Maxims of law:

The maxims of law are the immutable standards of law that are grounded in logic, reason, common sense, and truth. They are the foundational principals of law upon which all that is right, just, and true are founded. They are the standards used to measure the correctness and justice of any course of action. Maxims of law are the foundational principles of all written laws, which cannot be lawfully violated. The maxims of law govern common law jurisdiction, which stands paramount to all written laws and customs. Maxims are the rules of law and due process upon which people have the right to rely when protecting and defending their rights, liberties, freedoms, and property. The maxims of law have the power to cover every aspect of our lives and every topic imaginable without confusion or misunderstanding. Many of the pertinent maxims of law are stated below.

Pertaining to sovereignty
1. A free man has the natural right to do as his will dictates within the guidelines that he does not cause damage, create an obvious danger, or infringe upon the rights, liberties, or property of others.
2. It is self-evident that all men are endowed by their creator (God) with equal and unalienable rights.
3. The created cannot be greater than its creator.
4. A man can give to another no more than he himself has.
5. A man cannot give to anyone or anything any power or authority he does do not have.
6. A man may not with impunity infringe upon another man's rights.
7. No one has the right to force an obligation upon another with impunity.
8. The people of America are sovereign.
9. In America the government is the servant of the sovereign people.
10. Involuntary servitude of free, sovereign people is unlawful in America.

Pertaining to justice, due process, and the rule of law
11. A matter must be expressed to be resolved.
12. All are equal under the law.
13. The burden of proof of a claim that is compelling another to perform rests upon the party asserting the claim.
14. Claims made without accountability are void.

15. All presumptions of law are rebuttable.
16. A written law cannot lawfully or morally violate the rights of a free individual.
17. Failure to rebut a challenge, or silence to a challenge of a claim, results in forfeiture of right to that claim.
18. Silence is viewed as a tacit admission.
19. Might does not make right.
20. Thou shall not steal.
21. Force, perjury, or subornation of perjury, voids all.
22. A signature made under threat, duress, coercion, or force is not a valid signature.
23. Fraud vitiates the most solemn promise.
24. While the battle continues, he who first leaves the field of battle or refuses to contend loses by default.
25. A laborer is worthy of his hire.
26. Notice to agent is notice to principle. Notice to principle is notice to agent.
27. There must be a damage before there can be a crime or injustice. No harm, no foul.
28. Justice is determined by the preponderance of evidence.

Pertaining to truth
29. Truth is paramount and the objective of the rules of law.
30. Truth effects but cannot be affected.
31. Truth is expressed in the form of sworn affidavit or testimony.
32. An un-rebutted affidavit or testimony stands as the truth.
33. Rebuttal of an affidavit or testimony must be by sworn point-for-point testimony.
34. Sworn rebuttal of an affidavit or testimony creates a controversy.
35. Penalties for perjury are crucial elements in the due process of law.
36. Thou shall not bear false witness.

Logic dictates that when the maxims of law are followed, truth, justice, and fairness prevail in a high percentage of cases. Maxims of law can be used and understood by all people as easily as any common sense subject. It is virtually impossible to manipulate maxims of law in order to create fraud or injustice in the way that an attorney would manipulate written laws to cause confusion and create injustice. Any moral system of law mandates that maxims of law always hold precedence over written laws. Common sense tells us that any written law that violates a maxim of law is an oxymoron that is obviously in error, is an injustice and is unlawful.

Maxims of law have always been with us and will always be with us. They will never go away, just as logic, truth, and common sense will never go away. They can only be hidden through ignorance, deception, fraud, and oppression. Maxims of law are as important for people to know and understand as are reading, writing, and math. Maxims of law are an integral and essential part of any just and moral society. Without maxims of law there is only arbitrary corruption at the will of whatever master happens to rule with an iron fist or with stealthy hidden deception.

Know the maxims of law. Teach them to your children at an early age. Hang them on your wall in a nice frame. Never forget these important principles of law. For, if you do, you let your guard down to who ever wishes to oppress you, your family, or community. If you forget the maxims of law you are nothing more than an ignorant slave.

If you do not have any agreements or contracts with someone, then they cannot prove that you do. If they have no authority over you, then they cannot prove that they do. If you are not subject to their written laws or rules, than they cannot prove that you are. It is as simple as that, just as your common sense has told you.

Always remember, if you stick with the truth, the common law, the maxims of law and never waiver, give up, or bend to intimidation, then your truth will prevail in any honest and honorable court.

"God helps them that help themselves."
Benjamin Franklin

Building America Strong Again

Although many that love America say, "America is still the best country in the world," the fact of the matter is that America is in a hell of a mess, even if it is the best. This author has talked to many people who live in Europe who say that there is far more statutory oppression and intrusion in the private lives of Americans than in Europe. Even if it is true that America is the best country in the world, it does not hide the fact that America has serious problems that need remedy. You can live in the nicest house in a ghetto but it does not hide the fact that you are living in a ghetto. It does not hide the fact that you can improve the ghetto, or your home to a better standard of living.

At this time you can say that, in America, the more money you have, the more rights and liberties you have, partly because you have enough money to pay all the forced obligations.

If you are a man with minimal income to pay for the necessities of life, paying for the forced obligations, steals away your personal freedoms and liberties. So, in effect, forced obligations are more noticeable upon a poor man than a rich man. The rich man treats the forced obligation as an inconvenient business expense. But these forced obligations are rights violation to the poor man. They rob him of what he needs to survive and be happy. They rob the poor man of possessions that are his. They rob the poor man of his family, house, farm, vehicles, possessions, and freedoms with the government's self imposed impunity. They subject the poor man to nothing less than involuntary servitude. And this happens thousands of times a day throughout America.

If you have enough money to pay your taxes or hire powerful law firms, then you are able to win against those who don't have the money for powerful law firms, regardless of whether you are right or wrong. Just ask yourself this question: If you are right and lawful, why does it help to hire the best law firm to win? Why is it that a man with plenty of money to hire the most powerful law firm usually wins in court, even if he is in the wrong? Should it not be that the man who is in the right should win?

The reason is simply that the courts are more concerned about rules and regulations than justice, rights, freedoms, liberties, and maxims of law.

> *"The more laws, the less justice."*
> **Marcus Tullius Cicero De Officiis**

There are those who are down on their luck and are losing their homes because they are unable to pay their ever-increasing property taxes. There are old people who are losing the homes and farms they have lived in all their lives because they cannot afford property tax. There are those who are having their earnings, accounts, and property stolen by the IRS because they are unable to pay the extortion payments to the IRS. There are people going to jail and having their vehicles seized because they were cited for no license, registration, insurance, or even because they failed to have their seat belt buckled. There are people who are being forced to give their kids Ritalin, Dexedrine, and other harmful drugs because their kids seem different from other kids. The list goes on and on. The point is that we have a government that preys upon its people as if it were a sovereign, unjust master and the people are the citizen/slaves.

If we the people allow this presumption of legislative law to continue to oppress the people, some day it may be too late for our grandchildren to defend themselves according to American principles.

> *"When the well's dry, we know the worth of water"*
> **Benjamin Franklin**

Right now, we have to pay the government to live in our homes or have our homes stolen. We have to pay the government to work or have our accounts and property stolen. We have to pay the government to travel down the roadways or risk being thrown in jail and our vehicles seized. We have to pay the government to die in the form of inheritance tax. Does this sound like freedom and liberty to you?

Imagine if the government became so powerfully corrupt that it could force all people to submit to the will of the legislature. Imagine the government with complete political control over the people and the politicians that make the written laws, thereby forcing all people to submit to the will of the politically controlled legislature with punitive actions for noncompliance. Is it that hard to imagine now?

Right now the Supreme Courts are denying the people their due process on these very issues. They are doing their best to not have these important issues heard in court. Imagine if the Supreme Courts of the land became so blatantly corrupt that they literally forced legislative law down the throats of the people as if the Supreme Courts were the masters of the people. If this were to ever come about, America would fall headfirst into a hidden dictatorship in which the government would become the master of the people. Government employees would have more rights that private people because the people in government look after their own. And it would be likely that the people would still believe they live in a free country because they could take their chains off during certain times of the day.

Nazi Germany, Russia, Africa, China, Japan and North Korea are some prime examples of people being forced to submit to written law with no regard for their God-given rights or maxims of law. In a way, we are already there. The only difference is that the people have lawful recourse if they find out what their remedy is in time. America was founded on freedom and liberty of the people. The people of America have that fine, strong thread to hold on to. We had better start weaving this fine thread of liberty into a strong rope before it breaks.

The problem is that the people do not even realize how enslaved they are. They pay their last dime of survival money to the tax man and claim they are free. They are used to their involuntary servitude for the presumed good of the people. The tentacles of the invisible octopus of statutory oppression have almost completely enveloped the lives of the American people without their knowledge of it.

> *"Life without liberty is like a body without spirit."*
> **Kahlil Gibran**

Always remember this one immutable fact: If you are forced against your will to do anything, then you are no better than a slave and the authority that is forcing you is your master.

You may come up with excuses to convince yourself this is not true, but the fact is that it is.

If the people of America can wake up and realize the principles put forth here, there will be no more injustice caused by the government which was designed to protect us from injustice.

> *"We must all hang together, or assuredly we shall all hang separately."*
> **Benjamin Franklin**

Our economies will flourish when people can spend their hard earned money on things that will improve their lives instead of having it stolen from them. People will have more time to spend with their families when they are no longer forced to labor to pay government extortion payments. Truth and justice will once again become a reality in our everyday lives and courts of law. And just possibly our country will be printing United States Notes, which belong to the government instead of the private Federal Reserve Bank.

Remember this one important fact, the goal is to repair our government, not tear it down.

God will stand beside all of the brave people who exercise these principles of common law, freedom, and liberty. America will regain the strength and wisdom that our founding fathers fought so gallantly to create and preserve. God bless America and all people who have suffered and died for the cause of preserving and protecting true freedom and liberty.

> **"Resistance to tyranny is obedience to God."**
> **Thomas Jefferson**

You must remember that there are some basic principles of common law by which you must always live by. They are listed below for easy learning and future reference.

- The primary law of the people which dictates all and must be followed at all times, is this: It is your God-given inherent right to do as your will dictates as long as you do not create a damage, infringe upon the rights of others, or create an obvious danger to others. If everyone in the world abided by this simple maxim of law there could not be any injustice or crime in the world. If you live by this one simple law, everything in your life will turn for the better and you will be an asset to society. If you stand strong in defense of this law and influence your government and others to abide by this law you will be an asset to society. If you understand and abide by this one simple law, you understand *the law*.

- Understand the basic principle that no one has the right to force an obligation upon another with impunity. This should become second nature to you and all of your family. Always question any attempt to force obligations upon your rights. Remember that your money and possessions are a reflection of your labor, which are your rights. A forced obligation is involuntary servitude regardless of the name that is put on it.

- Read and understand the maxims of law listed in this book. There are many more, but the maxims in this book are some of the most important in everyday life. The point is not to necessarily memorize them. The point is to understand their meanings and to recognize when they are being violated and when they need to be implemented. Society's neglect of the maxims of law is the reason why things have gotten so far out of hand in the first place. The majority of Americans do not understand or recognize when maxims of law are being violated so America crumbles.

- Show as much good will as you can towards all without letting your good will negatively affect your survival. In other words, you can respect the rattlesnake for being one of God's creatures, but don't try to pet him. He bites. Understand that some people are dangerous. Wish them good will in your heart, but don't invite them for dinner or let them sleep in your bed.

- Always try to do the right thing, taking into consideration the maxims of law. If you always do the right thing you never have to look over your shoulder. Everything will work out right.

- Realize that when you waive your God-given rights against your will or consent for any reason, you are contributing to the problem of forced oppression upon society, which has almost ruined America and most countries of the world. It is the duty of all people to look after their own sacred rights and liberties. No one is expected to do it for you. No courts of law are bound to inform you of what your rights are. Courts are only supposed to support your rights if you claim them. "If you do not know what your rights are, you don't have any." There was never a truer statement.

- Understand that you can waive some of your rights, such as becoming incorporated, working for an employer, joining the military, getting licensed to do a business, etc. Understand the extent of the rights you are waiving according to your express consent and no more. Be watchful of encroachments into your life by unwarranted, forced obligations and legal trickery.

- Understand that all lawmaking bodies in America have only limited authority to make written laws, rules, and regulations that pertain to government and relating consenting commerce. No written law pertains to the private sovereign rights of the people absent their express or tacit consent. The legislature and lawmakers are not our king, master, or dictator. Further, they are just people with the job of operating and managing government. They hold absolutely no authority whatsoever over the private lives of individuals. Never allow this sacred maxim of law to be violated by your government. Fight it tooth and nail, as it determines the moral future and fabric of America and all societies of the world now and in the future.

- Do not fall into the mind-control trap that says that legislative laws will create justice or that they pertain to the private lives of people. Never assume that a written law was well thought out and just. There are individuals in government who wish to control the people like a herd of sheep, and they get paid well for doing so. These individuals want the people to believe their private lives are dictated by what the legislature enacts as statutes, laws rules, regulations, etc. If you are involved with some form of business or contract with government, understand just what rules and written laws pertain to you. Understand that it is all predicated upon your express consent.

- You are, as a private individual and human being, beholden and subject to the principles of common law, which includes all maxims of law. You cannot escape this. This is the law that you are beholden to, not statute or legislative laws. The common law is the law of all just societies and human beings. The common law is common sense and rational thinking.The maxims of law are the laws that bring us out of the animal world and regulate and maintain our morality and society.

- Help others who are attempting to protect their freedoms. When you help the cause of freedom and liberty, its goodness radiates out in all directions. Remember that true justice is obedience to maxims of law. It is impossible to create injustice when the maxims of law are obeyed. The more justice in a society, the more prosperous and productive that society is.

- Teach as many people as you can about this subject. Encourage others to read this book and others like it. If you never teach your children anything else, teach them the one simple law that is listed first above. Encourage your community colleges and universities to teach this simple subject to average people. Understand that, when all of society understands this subject as well as the average person knows how to read, then freedom and liberty will never again fall prey to the ignorance of man in understanding the law. Never again will governments be able to stealthily oppress the people without the people's knowledge of it. Never again will anyone be able to oppress anyone else with impunity. When this becomes reality, our societies will bloom and evolve to the next stage in human evolution.

The important thing to remember is that there will always be people in this world who will not understand, care about or even fear the principles of real law propounded in this book. There will be those who will say: "Oh my God! If we do not obey all the written laws there will be anarchy in the streets! We will not have schools and roads. Our government will collapse."

These are just fear-based, irrational delusions of people with an agenda or who are just plain ignorant. They may be people who cannot break old patterns or think "out of the box." Remember, it is impossible to have anarchy without violating maxims of law, not legislative law.

It is not necessary that everyone understands real law. It is necessary that the people who do understand have the right to exercise their sovereign freedoms and liberties according to the dictates of common law, all maxims of law, and due process. If there are people who wish to be slaves, let them. It is there right. As long as we have a society in which freedom and liberty is respected and understood, we will have a just society. For man to evolve out of the crime, war, oppression, and unjust mentality that have caused so much damage in the past, people only need to understand and implement this one true law of the people.

What Americans Need to Do
Now to Save America

The primary problems affecting the freedoms of Americans are very simply to understand. Understanding the problems in the simplest manner will enable the simplest of solutions to manifest. They are as follows:

1. The general erroneous misconception that government must force obligations or money from its citizens, in order to function.
2. The erroneous misconception that the people's private rights and freedoms are subject to the will of the legislature, written laws, and statutes.
3. The failure of people to understand the simple concepts of maxims of law, common law of the land, and due process.
4. The failure of the courts to respect the natural rights of the people, common law process and to abide by the principles of due process and the rule of law.

The first step to freedom: The misconception that government must force obligations or money from its citizens in order to function, and that the people's private rights and freedoms are subject to the will of the legislature, written laws, and statutes is the same myth that has caused tyranny to flourish throughout the ages. It is a simple trick used by governments to gain control of its citizenry. In other words, the government violates the rights of the people with the king's rules. It says the citizens must comply because the king said so. If you don't like it they will punish you.

This myth of trickery causes good, patriotic American people to be misguided into giving up their rights, freedoms, and liberties for what they believe is a worthy cause or patriotism. Allowing your rights to be usurped does nothing but ruin the moral and lawful fabric of a free society. It is important to understand that Americans do not have any kind of moral or lawful duty to give up any freedoms, liberties, properties, or rights. The government just forces the obligations upon the people because it has gotten away with it so far and the people put up with it.

This fabricated myth is the only argument government officials have mustered up to justify the usurpation of Americans rights and liberties. Any agreement to this myth is only out of ignorance, fear, coercion, or fraud. This myth is believed by many who have neither the time, nor inclination to think about the subject or even care. The truth of the matter is that freedom and liberty is the backbone of our American society and must never be waived under any circumstances, unless by one's express consent.

Anyone who intelligently and honestly contemplates this subject can readily determine that forcing obligations for any reason violates law. The same rules apply whether it is you or the government forcing obligations on somebody. It is sometimes hard to believe that government attorneys, officials, and judges tell people that they must comply with legislative law because it is the law. Especially judges, whose lawful duty it is to know and understand law as well as code pleading. When they are asked why the people may be subject to legislative rule, they merely skirt the issue and say, "Because it is dictated by the legislature." But they never respond to the real question asked: "Where did the legislature inherit the supreme right to make laws that can force obligations and violate the rights of private people?" They refuse to answer this all-important question. You will never hear any government official answer anything but "because it is the law." Government officials cannot answer this question because a truthful answer would deny them the presumed right to force the obligations upon private people. So government officials keep forcing the will of the legislature upon people and acting like they have the right to do so when, by law, they have no right to do so.

> **"The United States can't be so fixed on our desire to preserve the rights of ordinary Americans."**
> **Bill Clinton** (3-1-19 press conference, Piscataway, NJ. Boston Globe, 3-2-93, page 3)

Therefore, the very first part of the remedy for the people is to educate them that their private rights, freedoms, liberties, and property are not subject to anyone's will, let alone the government or the legislature. The fact must be realized that when no one can force obligations upon others, it will create more justice, fairness, and honor in society. A more just and free society creates more happiness and prosperity in the society. This is a logical fact that cannot be disputed by anyone of honest or sane intelligence. When this fact becomes common knowledge among the populace and media, the second step must be taken almost simultaneously.

The second step to freedom: Because the myth and fraud are ingrained so deeply among people and government, all government personnel are politically and financially motivated to keep forcing obligations upon the people and punishing those who resist. Government officials appear to erroneously believe that, if taxes and obligations are not forced upon people, government will not have money for their paychecks, pensions and to operate. All government employees actually have a real conflict of interest because they all receive their livelihoods from the government which is violating law by forcing the obligations upon the people. There is no one who works in any court system, law-enforcement system, or law-making body that does not receive compensation and benefit from the money extorted from the citizens by force. It is like a hidden war between government employees and private people. Of course government employees generally don't mind volunteering their rights because they truly believe their livelihood depends on forcing obligations upon others. Of course they would hold the erroneous contentions that if they have to contribute then everyone else must contribute as well. Otherwise their livelihood would fall apart.

When an individual sues the government for violating his rights and maxims of law, judges may deny the litigant due process and access to a fair trial by dismissing the case using statutory law ("The King said so"). It is the same method used over and over. The court merely says that it is dictated by statute and the written rules say that the litigant is not entitled to a trial on the issue. The case is dismissed on whatever technicality the court so desires. The judge just overlooks the fact that the litigant's right to due process of law is violated with legislative enactments. Besides, what is the litigant going to do if he can't get the issue in front of an informed jury? The judge knows that the litigant has no reasonable remedy or recourse in Amerika.

Since the police, judges, bailiffs, clerks, DA, attorneys, and most everyone else involved receives some type of benefit from the obligations forced upon the victim litigant, the litigant doesn't have a chance of receiving help or justice. So the litigant keeps bouncing around from court to court attempting to receive justice in a Catch-22 situation. Basically there is no remedy for the people at this time in today's courts and the people have no checks and balances against the government abuse. This is why the government has grown into such a powerful rights-gobbling monster.

The second step requires that many people start suing the government on the lawful principle that the people's rights are not subject to the will of the legislature and that the government has no right to force obligations upon the people. Get lots of media attention on these issues. Your case will make complete sense to anyone who cares to contemplate the issue. File complaints against all judges who do not make decisions according to law and the preponderance of evidence, and who deny litigants due process rights. Picket the court house if you have time. If Americans keep chipping away at it by the thousands, the remedy will come swiftly.

There will always be good, caring judges or competent, informed juries out there who will rule in favor of these obvious, lawful principles. Once the people have Supreme Court citations that dictate that people's rights are not subject to the will of the legislature, and that the people have the right to rely on maxims of law and due process to protect their rights, the problem is solved. All people who wish to defend their rights and liberties will be able to rely on these court citations for their litigations. The sad part of this whole thing is that this is the way real law is suppose to operate in the first place. Remember, if we lose the personal right to demand that government abides by the law of the people, then we have irrevocably lost our checks and balances on government and we are forever doomed into involuntary servitude.

The third step to freedom: Create a fail-safe system of checks and balances.

The third step is creating legislation and an amendment to the Constitution that clearly dictates rules to the government that people have the right to rely on maxims of law, due process, and common-law jurisdiction in the courts to protect their private rights. This will create written legislative laws that clearly dictate to the government its limitations when dealing with the private rights of the people. This amendment will safeguard the people's rights forever.

The only reason this amendment was not originally included in our Constitution is that our founding fathers never dreamed our government would weave such a web of hidden tyranny upon the people. How could they have ever dreamed or planned for such a complex system of fraud?

This third step will be the check that will remain in place for all time to ensure that government will never again slip into the present tyrannical methods it uses on people today. The importance of this safeguard is paramount; otherwise the same tyrannical methods will keep popping up just as they have popped up in tyrannical regimes since the beginning of time. It even appeared in the face of our own American Constitution and Bill of Rights.

A government that violates the rights of the people is contrary to a free society and government. You can not possibly have a just society when there is a self-imposed, supreme authority forcing obligations upon people and punishing them for non-compliance.

The Proper and Lawful Way for
Government to Operate

There are many ways for government to lawfully function financially. It is irrelevant that the government has become accustomed to extorting money from the citizens. Because the government has been extorting funds and forcing obligations for years does not make it lawful, moral, or compliant with due process or maxims of law.

The government can only legally tax through tariffs and trade (sales tax, alcohol tax, cigarette tax, fuel tax, etc.) through the consenting commerce, not to mention all of the other fees collected through commercial licensing, fees, fines, etc. This is the only way government is allowed to tax. The government has no lawful claims against the freedoms, liberties, and property of private people except to do justice to a convicted criminal.

The government must abolish the Federal Reserve Banking system (FED) and start printing United States Notes instead of Federal Reserve notes. (President Kennedy started the process and was shot two weeks after $5 dollar US notes were put into circulation.) The government will then lend the money into circulation (via the banks) so it will own and benefit from the money that is printed and lent into circulation instead of the privately owned FED. This was the original intent of our founding fathers. In this way all the money paid back will go into the government accounts instead of to the privately owned FED. The government will then owe nothing to the FED as it does now in the fraudulently conceived "National Debt."

Because the government would have no debt, it will have all the money it needs to operate. You have to remember that the money lent into circulation will be validated by the people when the loans are paid back. When you pay back a loan you pay it back with money you earned. You validated the money as a true reflection of your labor and services. All money is merely a tool for exchanging value.

With this new-found revenue source going to government instead of the privately owned FED, the government could fund public projects that would employ large Contractors who in turn would hire private people. When the government funds projects that benefit mankind and society, everyone wins. We could actually stimulate our economies with commerce instead of war.

This country does not need the unlawful system of allowing the private Federal Reserve Bank to own and control America's money supply. Besides, this system is repugnant to the Constitution. The FED puts up no gold for collateral when ordering Federal Reserve notes, or when lending the funds into circulation. The Federal Reserve Banks and affiliate lending institutions now receive the full benefit of the money lent into circulation without having to show any collateral at all or to pay for the money. They get the money for free and lend it to government and people. The money lent to the government is called the national debt. All of the money paid back goes into the accounts of the Federal Reserve banking system instead of the United States Treasury as it should according to the Constitution and by all rights. It is a sweet deal for the FED and a bad deal for American government and the people. It is the biggest fraud ever perpetrated in the history of the world.

Our government must realize that by the law of our Constitution, our government must own and control its own money system by producing United States Notes instead of Federal Reserve Notes. This was of the utmost importance to our founding fathers and Lincoln. This is why our founding fathers dictated in the Constitution that only congress shall mint and coin money and regulate the value thereof (Art. I, sec. 7, cl. 5). They did not intend for Congress to mint and coin money for a private bank (the FED).

There is nothing wrong with the practices of lending money into circulation and minting money that is not backed by gold. There is not enough gold in the world to back all currencies. In fact, lending printed money into circulation creates prosperity because there are unlimited funds available. You have to remember that money is only a tool used to exchange value just like the deed to your house or title to your car. It is a reflection of your labor and service. Money is merely a note or a promise to pay. The government must receive the benefit of creating the money instead of private world banks (FED) or the system is flawed and impossible to fix. Just like and airplane with a missing wing.

If the Treasury receives the benefit of creating the money supply there is no need or excuse to force obligations upon the people with the myth that the government will go broke if we don't do something drastic like usurp your rights and property. The government will own all money in America, will have no debt, and will have all the money needed to function. More money than the private International Monetary Fund.

We have to understand that although our founding fathers were intelligent, honorable, and inspired men, they were only human. They gave us our start. It would have been impossible for them to see the future and create a perfect Constitution that would have prevented the current fraud upon the people. Remember they were young, writing under candle light, no air conditioning, with no white out or erasers while fighting the most powerful military in the world. I think they did pretty darn good considering.

It is now up to us to take this great country into the future and set examples of freedom and liberty for the whole world. It is the time and place to create a fail-safe system of preserving the rights of the people forever. When it is done, our forefathers will rest in peace.

The solution at a glance:
1. Educate the people and government that no one has the right to force obligations upon others and that the legislature and the written laws have no authority over the private rights, freedoms, liberties, and properties of the people.
2. Sue the government on the principles of law that the rights of the people are not subject to the will of the legislature and that due process rights must be honored in all courts of law in the land. Establish such Supreme Court citations on which the people can rely.

3. Enact legislation amendments to the Constitution that clearly dictate rules that say that government cannot force obligations upon the people, and that people have the right to rely on maxims of law, due process, and common law jurisdiction in the courts to protect their private rights.

4. Cause the government to abolish the Federal Reserve System and start printing United States Notes instead of Federal Reserve Notes. The government must hold full ownership of the country's money supply; otherwise the private banks will continue to control our government.

Conclusion

Happiness is the goal in our lives. The end result of everything that we do is happiness and comfort. People are happier when no one is violating the rights of others and there is justice in society. If we succeed in the effort to free America again, America will once again become a lawful society at its finest and will inspire the entire world. If we fail, we will only fall deeper into despotism.

This is why we cannot allow government to violate maxims of law and the rights of people. The people are the only check on all three branches of government. It is just a long-forgotten process and practice that the people must become re-accustomed to. This is why the people have the right to enforce authority over government when it is proven that maxims of law are being violated. The people have the right to enforce due process and maxims of law in the court systems using simple common law, regardless of whether bad judges tell us this right has been legislated away. To deny people these rights is to sever all ties with freedom, liberty, and justice.

Not allowing your government to violate rights, due process, and maxims of law is imperative to developing a lawful and just society and government. The charge that the government violates civil and private liberties is always to be considered a most serious charge.

The ways of nature tells us that all the great answers will come in the simplest possible form. It does not get any simpler than this. So let's make this world and country a better place to live.

> *"The ultimate measure of a man is not where he stands in moments of comfort, but where he stands at times of challenge and controversy."*
>
> **Martin Luther King Jr.**

Prudent Warning to the People

Officials of the United States government are forcing more and more obligations upon the private rights of people on a regular and methodical basis. The courts are denying people due process of law when they attempt to assert their rights in court. Whether they are doing it with malice or out of ignorance, it makes no difference because it is happening. This is self-evident by all the fees, taxes, fines, rules, regulations, and punishments that are being forced upon the American people. This is happening because most people do not know how or they are afraid to stand up to the powerful presence of the government. This is understandable as we are all concerned about the survival of ourselves and our loved ones.

Keep in mind that if we do not stand up now, if we continue to allow officials in government to force obligations upon us with impunity, America and perhaps the entire world will eventually fall into total feudalism. America, founded on the principles of true freedom and liberty, will only be a shell of its original intent. Our grandchildren will grow old subject to involuntary servitude and punishment for those who dare to resist or rebel. And if this comes to pass, it will be our own fault.

Our founding fathers are watching us now, wondering how complacent the people of America will become. Will America fall just as every other country in the world has fallen at one time or another? Will some Americans act like the loyalists in the revolutionary war? You have a choice; will you allow obligations to be forced upon you? Will you witness maxims of law being violated and do nothing? Or will you make your personal stand to protect your own freedoms and liberty at any cost, just like our forefathers who created this great country? Are we going to dishonor everything our forefathers sacrificed for the founding principles of this country? Will you have the guts to utter the words, "Who are you and do I have some kind of agreement with you" "Prove your claim" the next time anyone attempts to force an obligation upon you? It is your choice, to allow maxims of law to be violated, or stop the violation in its tracks.

Remember, learning these simple concepts of freedom and law are as simple as learning the alphabet and reading. You just have to learn the basics and the rest falls right into place through your common sense and reasoning. The law is meant to be simple for the people to use.

Imagine a world in which the long forgotten principles of law propounded in this book became common knowledge among all people. This is not rocket science! Imagine if people did not lose their possessions and family homes because they could not pay their property taxes. Imagine a world where there was no government oppression or forced obligations. Imagine our government printing its own money instead of bank notes of a private bank. Imagine if all people understood and lived by the principles of common law and instinctively knew when a maxim of law was violated. Imagine the productivity of the human race with no wars or rights violations. Imagine all of society evolving to the next step in the evolution of humanity.

Just imagine and now make it a reality!

> *"The people are the only sure reliance for the preservation of liberty"*
>
> **Thomas Jefferson**

www.ingramcontent.com/pod-product-compliance
Lightning Source LLC
Chambersburg PA
CBHW030806180526
45163CB00003B/1166